Performance Through The Dance Technique of Lester Horton

Bradley Shelver

Forward by Ana Marie Forsythe

Photographs by Torben Rasmussen

ISBN: 148239278X
ISBN-13:978-1482392784

INTRODUCTION

This Book is a culmination of 13 years of study of the Horton Technique. It has been a wonderful journey to rediscover the rich heritage and wonderful structure and possibilities of this beautifully designed technique.

Ms. Francesca Falcone, who had a wonderful idea to bring together a series of dance books concerned with the history and methods of technique and performance first approached me in 2006. I wanted to be clear that my interest, although in the technical side of dance, would be primarily performance based. I wanted to write about my experiences and ideals for not only the Horton Technique, but for dance in general. It is my feeling that dance, and certainly the dancer should not be limited to one style or one technique, but be able to consider him or herself simply a movement artist and in my studies and interviews of the Horton technique, I discovered what a versatile and creative training tool it was. I want to pass my passion, experience and ideas on to a new generation of dance student, and distil the sense of heritage that is American modern dance. Horton was certainly a gift to me, and through my early training with masters like Milton Myers and Ana Marie Forsythe, my dedication and interest in the technique has grown.

I have always said that it is important to give your body somewhere to come from in order for it to know where it is going, and what it is expected to achieve. It was my aim in this book to bring together the history, creativity and possibilities encouraged by Lester Horton, and hopefully show the future of dance performance training to be a bright and adventurous one. I will always be a student, I will always be a dancer, I will always be a teacher, therefore I will always be learning and evolving. This has been **my** path and **my** experience with the technique of Lester Horton. It is a clear, powerful, musical and engaging journey and through it I have always been encouraged to find my own teaching style and where some might disagree, I hope others will find some insights and hopefully discover the passion and joy which is the Horton technique.

CONTENTS

FORWARD BY ANA MARIE FORSYTHE

Bradley Shelver, because of his exceptional potential and talent was personally selected by Judith Jamison, Artistic Director of the Alvin Ailey American Dance Theater, to come to The Ailey School as a special scholarship recipient in 1998. As a student at The Ailey School, Bradley took classes in ballet, Graham-based modern, Horton technique, West African and jazz. After all these years, Bradley continues to be a serious and highly motivated student, but now he is one who has grown into a technical, versatile and passionate dance artist and teacher.

In 1990 I co-authored a book, <u>The Dance Technique of Lester Horton</u>, with Marjorie B. Perces and Cheryl Bell, which remains the only written documentation of the Horton Technique. The book describes Horton studies and continues to be a resource for the numerous Horton teachers throughout the world. In my forty years of teaching at The Ailey School, I have helped begin the careers of a large number of Horton teachers.

From the beginning of our teacher /student relationship, I was always aware of Bradley's intelligence and curiosity about Horton technique, so it came as no surprise when he informed me 3 years ago that he was planning to write a book about his experiences as a Horton teacher and dancer. I feel Bradley brings a unique perspective to dance not only because of his versatile dance training but because of the varied companies he has worked with as dancer, choreographer and teacher; companies like Ailey II, The Jose Limon Dance Company, the Elisa Monte Dance Company, Complexions Contemporary Ballet, Phoenix Dance Theater, Metropolitan Opera Ballet, among others. He has built an understanding of how the body works through exploration of his own body's abilities and through his keen observations of how the body moves. There are inevitably different perspectives on teaching particular aspects of dance technique- in some areas I share Bradley's perspective, while in other areas my views differ. For Example, In Bradley's experience in the teaching of Horton as a company class, he has found it necessary to intersperse the technique with elements of other styles and modern dance schools, I have however found that a pure Horton class can also be exceptionally beneficial to professional dancers who are beginning to learn the

technique. However, I do feel he has explored his topic with seriousness and thoughtfulness. He brings a fresh voice to the issue of training dancers for the next generation and he is forward-looking about the future of the technique.

I believe Lester Horton was not only a genius, but continues to be one of the most influential modern dance pioneers. Horton created an enduring technique which was based on the principal of creating a movement vocabulary which was anatomically corrective and one that would build the body up, not tear it down. I am pleased to see the technique used by many teachers and choreographers.

Bradley has written a loving and an insightful discussion of the Horton technique. This book is a welcome contribution to the limited existing writings about the Lester Horton's modern dance technique.

Ana Marie Forsythe

ACKNOWLEDGMENTS

This work could not have been possible without the persistence and dedication of Francesca Falcone, who gave me the possibility and idea for this book. I want to thank Larry Warren, the insightful and devout author of Horton's Biography, for providing the source and depth of Lester Horton's life for us to be able to understand the man better.

I would like to thank Ana Marie Forsythe from the Ailey School whose guidance, knowledge and contributions to my work have been invaluable. Her book, The Dance Technique of Lester Horton, co-authored with Marjorie B. Perces and Cheryl Bell has made all the most difficult investigation, manageable. I would like to thank Ms. Judith Jamison of the Alvin Ailey American Dance Theater for her support and nurturing. I would like to thank Milton Myers, a clear inspiration and a focused force in my understanding of Horton's technique. A big supporter in my creative process as a teacher and choreographer, The Ailey School, the official school of the Alvin Ailey American Dance Theater, a continued and bright beacon for the dissemination of the principals and possibilities of the Horton Technique.

I would also like to thank Victor See Yeun and William Catanzaro, both accomplished and dedicated musical artists who's thoughts and incredible playing have inspired my classes and students.

The Photographs could not have been possible without the beautiful contributions of Danish Photographer and artist, Torben Rasmussen and dancer and model for the photographs, Mette Rasmussen. The research and insights could not have been possible without the help of Valerie Ifill from the University of Oregon, Dr. David Carless from Leeds Met University in the UK and Ms. Carmen de Lavelade who inspired myself, and an entire generation of modern dancers through her beauty, grace and understanding of Mr. Horton.

I would like to thank my family. My father, Clive Shelver, Pauline and Klair for their love and support. Stacy Donnelly whose support helped me to think clearly. Lastly, I would like to thank every student and dancer that has trusted me enough to have me guide and challenge them.

.

CHAPTER 1:
A BRIEF INTRODUCTION TO LESTER HORTON

" A genius on the wrong coast" wrote the American critic, Clive Barnes of Lester Horton in the Los Angeles Herald Examiner on December 3rd 1967[1]. His life's work and dedication to the creation of not only dances, but also dancers and artists was in my opinion the work of a creative genius.

Lester Horton was born on January 23rd, 1906, in Indianapolis, Indiana. The son of Iredell Horton and Annie Lauders (also known as Poly Anna), the family moved often, as many as Four times before Horton was five years old. The final move was to the farm area of Brazil, Indiana, near Terre Haute. A tranquil, southern landscape which Horton apparently often spoke of in his later life, and it's effect on his work. His father, Iredell worked as a laborer, custodian and park attendant but his drinking prevented him from bringing in enough funds for the family to survive. His early years spent in this area were a continuous voyage of discovery for the youngster and he was often described as bright, cheerful and well behaved. Although sometimes an overly emotional child, he possessed a kind of magnetism. After World War 1, the family decided to move back to the city of Indianapolis, Horton was 12 years old and was tremendously exited by city life. He joined the library's Nature Study Group where he was taken on many excursions to the American Indian landscapes. As a student at Short Ridge High School, he showed a keen interest in the arts of science, nature and American Indian history and culture, The Children's Museum of Meridian Street became his second home and he had announced to his family he would grow up to be a herpetologist (a specialist in that branch of Zoology which deals with reptiles and amphibians).

Having an enquiring mind and an interest in the arts, his ideas for the development of movement and its expressive capabilities came at age 16 from an early performance of the Denishawn Dancers in December 1922 at the Murat Theater in Indianapolis. The program included Ted Shawn's Aztec ballet, Xochitl and a cast comprising of Charles Weidman, Martha Graham and Doris Humphrey – who with Horton were to become the cornerstones of American modern dance. The program included theatricalized dances inspired by the dance forms of India, Siam, Japan, Java and Egypt and the exotic

---

Lester Horton, Modern Dance Pioneer- Larry Warren, Pub. M.Dekker (1977)

The company was founded 1915 in Los Angeles by Ted Shawn and Ruth St Denis.

movements and splendor of the costumes evoked the idea in his mind that he had to be apart of the magic on the stage, he had to dance! The power, grace, and passion of the Denishawn Dancers[2] prompted the curious Horton to study dance with Mlle Theo Hewes, a student of the east coast teacher, Madame Menzeli, who had received her fame from her production of The Black Crook[3]. Mlle Hewes trained Horton in the Italian Ballet method however Horton's body was not designed for the classical technique and so he disliked the physical discipline it required of him. Horton also found time to take art courses at the Herron Art Institute in Indianapolis where he studied Greek classical art and movement aesthetics but found himself drawn to the theater, and began work with the Indianapolis Little Theater where he did work in production and design. He started teaching sporadically for Mlle Hewes where he developed his first taste for dance education. He also began creating his own American Indian dances, which, he based on authentic materials and which contained a theatrical element inspired by his design, and theater training he was receiving at the Little Theater.

While still at school he developed a fascination for drawing, pottery and jewelry making and his fascination and talent for costume and set design seemed to be prevalent in his works, throughout his career and he eventually dropped out of high school and continued pursuing his interest in learning Indian stories, songs and chants. In 1925, American choreographer, Forrest Thornburg[3A] gave him his first experience as a professional with a touring company. Thornburg taught Horton some Denishawn dances, and Horton in turn assisted the choreographer in rehearsals. It was in this year that Lester began studies in Chicago, with ballet master, Adolph Bolm[4] however Horton

The company was founded 1915 in Los Angeles by Ted Shawn and Ruth St Denis.

[3] *The Black Crook* which premiered at the Niblo's Garden Theatre, New York, on the 12th September 1966 and is considered to be the first piece of musical theatre that conforms to the modern notion of a "book musical". The book is by Charles M. Barras (1826-1873), an American playwright. . It is choreographed by David Costa with music by Thomas Baker. The exact Date of her production was unavailable at print.

[3A] Mr. Thornburg later went on to establish the Nashville Civic Ballet

[4] Adolph Bolm (1884-1951) Russian- American dancer, teacher and choreographer was admitted to the Imperial Ballet School, at age ten, then he entered the corps de ballet of the Maryinsky Theater, becoming a soloist. He collaborated with Ballets Russes- 1909-

endured only 2 lessons in the Russian ballet method as he found Mr. Bolm to strict a task master.[4B]

The formation of The Indianapolis Theater Guild by William and Clara Nixon Bates[5] in the 1920's provided Horton with his first opportunity to choreograph. Ms Bates had a keen interest in Indiana history and perhaps inspired by Ted Shawn's idea in his 1926 book, The American Ballet, Horton set about to do a production on Longfellow's poem, The Song Of Haiwatha. Ms. Bates initial meeting with Horton was at the Little Theater Costume ball. She had heard about a gifted young man at the Theo Hewes School and invited him to meet her for tea. His interview with her went well, and he spoke intelligently and thoughtfully. She was impressed by his knowledge of the artifacts in her extensive collection of Indian drums, rattles, blankets and pottery. The two got along well, and agreed to work together on the project. Ms. Bates had learnt a great deal about production, promotion and fundraising during her years as an active member of the Little Theater. She got the organization into full swing, recruiting dancers, musicians and helpers of all kinds, including the most important- sponsors. After naming Horton as Art Director and Dance Master of the guild, she invited him to participate in an expanded version of the work in which he would play the leading role, be responsible for the lighting, and did much of the costume design and its execution. The production made short tours to the Midwest of the United States.

In July 1928, Ms. Bates arranged with Mrs. J.E Argus from Eagle Rock, California, another socialite and arts philanthropist, to present the work at the Argus Bowl, a natural amphitheater on the family estate. The Song of Hiawatha became Horton's first choreographic

---

1917, as a most prominent male dancer, after Nijinsky. Partner to Anna Pavlova in Diaghilev's Ballet Russe between 1909-1917 He left the company and settled permanently in the United States, where he formed an ensemble (Ballet Intime) where he created numerous choreographies.

[4B] Lester Horton: Modern Dance Pioneer. Larry Warren. Page 11

[5] Socially prominent philanthropists, Clara Bates had for several years been producing a music, dance and drama pageant based on Longfellow's poem, The *Song of Hiawatha*. She and her husband supported young writers, especially when the subject matter was indigenous.

work. The production of Hiawatha received mixed reviews, Redfern Mason, a critic for the San Francisco Examiner, was impressed: " The words are Longfellow's; the music is tribal from coast to coast; the dances and ceremonies are authentic...it was like slipping away from the workday world into that folk life which is the primitive poetry of America".[5A] About 25 performances of the pageant were given in California over the next few years and excerpts and themes of the material would stay in Horton's repertory for many years. The working relationship between Clara Bates and Horton[5B], after the death of her husband continued for many years and she was instrumental in his fist experience with staging and choreographing.

The following year, in 1929, Japanese born choreographer and teacher, Michio Ito[6] who produced what he called, "plays for dancers", invited Horton to join his company. Ito often choreographed to the music of Schumman, Beethoven, Borodin and Debussy and perhaps introduced this classical genre to the young Horton. That year, Horton received his first lead role in Ito- Yeate's, *At the Hawk's well*[7]. From Ito, his most influential teacher, Horton learned stage projection, and the extensive and intrinsic use of props. His movement style highlighted the use of the upper body, head, shoulders and particularly arms, all of which were to form a focal point in the Horton technique later on. Horton toured with Ito for 2

[5A] Starting from Indiana by Larry Warren. Dance Perspectives 31, Autumn 1967 Page 5

[5B] Horton's professional name for a short time during this period was, Okoya Tihua- an American Indian name from Mythology.

[6] Michio Ito 1892c. -1961, Japanese exponent of American Modern Dance. During his time at the Emile Jaques-Dalcroze Institute at Hellerau, near Dresden, he began to formulate his own technique. Ito moved to New York City in 1916 and opened a Studio in 1919. His teaching and methodology influenced Ted Shawn, Martha Graham, Pauline Koner, Lester Horton and Luigi among others. Ito created a unique East and West synthesis that gave legitimacy to cross-cultural choreography. He was the choreographer of the *Garden of Kama* in which Martha Graham made her 1923 debut in the Greenwich Village Follies.

[7] *At the Hawk's Well* is a one-act play by William Butler Yeats, first performed in 1916 and published in 1917. Ito assisted Ezra Pound in editing Ernest Fenollosa's new manuscripts, and he joined Pound and William Butler Yeats in the production of At the Hawks, Yeats's new style of play.

years and occasionally presented his own choreography on these programs. Ito's experience with actors also provided Horton his first experience in the process of creating what was to be called the "Chore drama"[8] which possibly developed from Ito's, "plays for dancers" idea. Years later Horton would be involved in creating works which brought not only technical prowess but a true sense of dramatic artistry and intention, he would be considered a showman in the dance theater genre.

In 1932, Glendale High School teacher Jean Abel[8A] gave Horton his first teaching experience when she invited him to direct and choreograph an Indian Pageant[8B] and share classes with her for the summer course at the Little Theater of the Verdugos, northeast of Glendale California. Having very little experience as a dancer and teacher at that early stage, his students described his classes as being difficult and demanding of endurance, flexibility and strength, and were often afraid they would not survive the two-hour sessions. Horton's first attempt at dance class seemed to lack structure and flow but, after researching some basic anatomy, he seemed to improve in the way he was designing the warm-ups and began to emphasize the importance of including breath and transitions into his movements.

When Horton began teaching Saturday morning classes at the Norma Gould[9] studio in Los Angeles, the Verdugos students would travel up to continue their training with him. This became the nucleus for the Lester Horton Dance Group.

The appearance on the dance scene of German born dancer and

---

[8] Music with movement to portray a message it is a blend of drama, mime and choreographed movement. Not just for trained dancers.

[8A] Ms Able had the prior year described Horton's production of *Haiwatha* as, " not really very much of anything- dull as a matter of fact". Lester Horton: Modern Dance Pioneer- L. Warren. Page 23

[8B] A narrative procession connected with a festival, making use of elaborate costumes in a public display.

[9] Miss Gould was Ted Shawn's first dance partner and coined the name "Dance Theater" which Horton later used.

choreographer, Mary Wigman[10], that same year, further sparked Horton's creative ideals and he closely observed her use of percussion instruments as motivation for new dance ideas. Her influence can be found in his swing combinations and his endless fascinations with turns. His studies in ancient and traditional dances and movements inspired the creative energy and concepts in his work and his technique and in 1932, the Lester Horton Dancers appeared for the first time at the Olympic Festival of the dance at the Los Angeles Philharmonic Auditorium. For the event Horton presented *Voodoo Ceremonial*, which was inspired by American author William Buehler Seabrook's book on Haiti, The Magic Island. As well as, *Kootenai War Dance* (American Indian). Horton's collection of instruments from American Indian and other cultures over the span of his life was quite considerable, and the use of percussive scores and accompaniment in his choreography and classes provided him with a continuing link to these cultures that had interested him throughout his early life. The success of this first performance led to a weeklong season at the Paramount Theater in Los Angeles. Horton's name was beginning to spread.

In 1934, a young and feisty dancer by the name of Bella Lewitzky[11] enrolled in Lester Horton's classes. She was a physically well-equipped dancer, who brought enthusiasm and commitment to dance. Although Horton himself was an excellent performer particularly in demi-character roles, he was not physically well designed for dance. He was short and stocky, with a barrel-chested torso and short legs and his endurance and personal range for movement were limited[12]. In Ms Lewitzky, Horton saw a perfect vehicle for the realization of his vision of dance, he trusted her, and she inspired him. In 1934, Horton was invited to direct Oscar Wilde's, *Salome* at the Little Theater of the Verdugos. Under his direction, dance was

---

[10] Mary Wigman born Karoline Sophie Marie Wiegmann in 1886 – 1973. She is credited for innovation of expressionist dance, and pioneer of modern dance in Germany. Her work in the United States is credited to her protogee' Hanya Holm, and then to Hanya's students Alwin Nikolais and Joanne Woodbury.

[11] Lewitzky was born in 1916 in Los Angeles. She left the Horton organization in 1950 to pursue her own career and founded the Lewitzky Dance Company in 1966.

[12] Starting from Indiana, by Larry Warren. Dance Perspectives 31, Autumn 1967. Page 10

incorporated and the production won a Los Angeles County Drama Association award. One reviewer described it as a "verbal ballet", again an indication of his growing ability in the creation of theater dance and the production was expanded later that year for a run at the grand, "Shrine Auditorium". The program for the Shrine included Horton's, Painted Desert Ballet and Chinese Fantasy as well as a work by Horton company member; Brahm Van den Berg called, *American in Paris*. Salome was immensely well received with Horton himself playing the role of Herod. At this stage, Horton would seemingly get ahead of his own development as a choreographer and over estimated the technical abilities of most of his performers. He liked to use large numbers of people on stage, and often utilized dancers that were not ready for viewing by audiences. Although the reviews were mostly enthusiastic and encouraging, they also criticized some of the work for being repetitive, pretentious and affected. In the mid 1930's, Lewitzky and another dancer, Eleanor Brooks[13], encouraged Horton to remove the excessive trappings of theater and pageantry. They encouraged him to clarify the theatrical intentions of his work and his training technique and, Horton's 1935 ballet, *Mound Builders* ,(begun the previous year under the name Aztec Ballet), saw a trend developing in his work.

Before 1935, Horton had not expressed a choreographic interest in the turmoil of the Depression and the development of left-wing organizations within the US. In the sections of Mound Builders known as "Dance for Zapata" and "Dance into Solidarity", Horton's interest in the social and political desperation of this era became apparent. In Mound Builders we notice a shift into more contemporary concerns in both his subject matter, and the choreographic treatment thereof. Horton began to emerge as a choreographer intensely aware of the problems of his time. It was also a recognizable move into the thematic materials for his works called *Conquest* (also called,! *Tierra y Libertad*!), a development of Horton's choreographic exploration of Mexico's turbulent past and *Chronicle*, an epic of American themes starting with the conquest of the Indians through the American Civil War. For the next several years, ballets such as *The Dictator* and *The Mine* would appear on his programs and

---

[13] Ms Brooks danced in the films *White Savage* (1943) and *Rhythm of the Islands* (1943) as a Horton dancer.

company members who shared his social views or concerns either stayed, or quietly moved on.

During the late 30's, the companies of Dorris Humphrey and Martha Graham appeared on the West coast of the United States and were received with great enthusiasm. At first Horton tried to stay away from their performances for fear of assimilating too much of their style and thereby loosing his own creativity. It however became impossible, and his admiration and curiosity for these pioneers overwhelmed him. Many believe he incorporated some of their early principles into his technique if so, they certainly became " Hortonized", and he was quoted as saying," The body will understand what the mind wants it to do, and will be responsive if you don't think so much"[14]. Certainly he was never accused of over thinking his creativity but it is understandable that he wanted to maintain the integrity of his ideas while still being open to the foundations being laid by others in the field. Although being very imaginative in his artistry, he was not shy in borrowing titles of ballets from other major choreographers, such as his 1937 ballet, *Chronicle*, which got its name from an earlier work by Martha Graham. Whether Horton was aware of this fact still remains disputed. Horton was evolving a distinctive style of movement that drew less and less from the main stream of modern dance development and more to his own creative fertility. Horton created a suite of ten or more dancers entitled, *Something to Please Everybody* in 1939. The work varied in style and theme and changed in order and number with each performance. It was a light-hearted break from his epic and often heavy, choreographic story lines of this period. Being on the West Coast it is important to mention that of all the influential and ground breaking choreographers of his era; Horton was not in a region or ethos where he had direct exchange of ideas with artists of his own stature. He was building a company in a climate that was mostly influenced by commerciality and where dance was perceived as entertainment- not a vehicle for the voicing of social injustice or change. *Something to Please Everybody* was perhaps his attempt at recognizing the importance of reaching his audiences on a different level and accepting the fundamental thought behind theater, that of entertainment.

---

[14] "The Dance Theater of Lester Horton"By: Larry Warren, Frank Eng, Bella Lewitzky and Joyce Trisler ,Dance Perspectives 31, Autumn , 1967 Page 17

In 1936, with the growing success of his work, The Lester Horton Dance Group moved into there own studio at 7377 Beverly Blvd. in Los Angeles. Horton was himself involved in classes for company members and they centered around current events, including history of art, music and dance, scene design, make-up and partner support. When a new work was created and inspired by a particular culture, the art, history and movement would be studied, offering the dancers a greater awareness and connection to these themes. In 1936, Horton created *Lysistrata* that became a further development of his concept of choreodrama[14A], which he had started with his production of Salome. Here he used the principal characters to tell the story and did away with the use of large groups for the sake of creating spectacle. The use of fewer dancers on stage was to be a sign of Horton's deepening artistic maturity. Horton's 1937 production of *Le Sacred u Printemps* (The Right of Spring) was scheduled for an August debut at the Hollywood Bowl. With only 2 orchestra rehearsals, the performance was met with audiences, shouting, catcalling and demanding refunds during the performance. The public was expecting a ballet and was not use to the barefoot, angular, sensual and unfamiliar movements of the dancers. The score by Russian born, Igor Stravinsky was harmonic and rhythmically exiting but was demanding on the ear. Critics however like Viola Hegyi Swisher a reviewer for the Hollywood Citizen News found the production "undeniably forceful" with "sequences of power and primitive beauty".

Despite the hesitation of audiences to his new production, the critics were positive and as Horton's confidence in his choreographic abilities grew, so did the structure of his classes and he believed in the value of improvisation. His classes were built on progressions and consisted of a short warm up. His whole class was designed around exploring a single movement idea and he would demonstrate a phrase and the dancers would vary the movement, therefore classes were never the same. This was also how he choreographed. His work with Ito led Horton into developing his own upper body vocabulary including rolling actions through the spine and undulations in the torso and pelvis. It was important for him that it did not resemble balletic movement and therefore, he focused on second and fourth

---

[14A] Defined as a drama expressed in dance or with dance as an integral part of its content and form.

positions of the legs taking its architecture from East Indian sculpture and dance which had emphasis on the arms and hands. The school of the Horton Dance Group began to develop a strong reputation in the area, and company members taught all the classes. The school offered music for dance, speech, orchestration and dance composition with special classes for men, actors and teachers. Through her work in the school, Horton company member Bella Lewitsky[15], who often criticized Horton for being careless in his class structures, brought more format, shape and clarification to his movement studies. Horton however felt her teaching style was too balletic and curbed the student's spontaneity but, despite their differences, she was an intricate driving force behind the development of his technique. The combination of his creativity and her desire for form created a powerful training tool for dancers and students alike, around the studio it was said that, " if Bella can't do it, it can't be done"[16]. With her ideas in mind, Horton began to consider the human body and its strengths and limitations; this however did not deter him from demanding more of his dancer's stamina. He began to develop a technique that was more mindful of the body, and therefore more streamlined, allowing him to train dancers in a shorter amount of time. The technique had no style; in the sense the word has today. A Horton dancer had no mannerisms, but instead could be recognized by high extensions and a flexible back.

He began to derive exercises for every part of the face, fingers and toes. He focused on joint actions in the body and correcting physical faults and combined these with an artistic design and an understanding of the origins of the movement. These primitive movements that he had studied from a young age, and the directions they could be taken in, became the bases of his technique. There was a great emphasis on performance, both qualitatively and technically: his was a technique of performance. In addition to the purely technical exercises, there were long combinations that made use of dramatic motivation. An example is the "Guernica Study"[17], Inspired

---

[15]Later she was to be given credit as co-choreographer on several of his ballets.

[16] The Magic and Commitment. By Joyce Trisler. Dance Perspectives 31, autumn 1967. Page 56

[17] This study was later incorporated into his dance dedication to Hiroshima.

by Picasso's mural. It was the study of a person in shock and combined dramatic requirements with that of great technical demand. With time, his focus became clearer and more isolated, movements of the pelvis became important; he also began to focus on developing exercises from swinging movements. Sharp and clear rib isolations were introduced and slow movements influenced by Japanese Theater Dance were refined and added. The style, through its elevations and fast movements and imbued with masculine grandeur, became a lyrical technique[18] demanding not only strength, stamina and power, but also fluidity, musicality and artistic sensitivity. Horton did not want to create dancers with a "Horton look" but instead was keen on designing versatility through creativity in his dancers.

Horton was quoted in saying, " I am sincerely trying to create a dance technique based entirely on corrective exercises, created with a knowledge of the human anatomy, a technique that will correct faults and prepare a dancer for any type of dancing he may wish to follow, a technique having all the basic movements which govern the actions of the body, combined with the knowledge of the origins of the movements and a sense of the artistic design". [19]In my opinion he succeeded in his mission, having established a technique for both dancers and choreographers and was responsible for training and influencing modern dance pioneers such as Alvin Ailey, Janet Collins[20], Carmen De Lavallade, Bella Lewitzky, James Mitchell, Joyce Trisler and James Truitte. Ms. Lewitzky said of Horton's technique, " We felt that the body itself was a determining factor, and that it should be developed in as many ways as needed by a choreographer. So we set about to broaden the technique, rather than limit or even define it". " Our entire vocabulary in those days was fashioned out of exploration on the part of the company, then Lester would draw from what we had done, guiding us towards the things he felt were significant and welding them into technical studies". [21] Many

---

[18] Lyrical movement refers to an expressive and deeply felt quality. It could have the sense of an adagio, but with a dynamic quality.

[19] Starting from Indiana, by Larry Warren. Dance Perspectives 31, Autumn, 1967 Page 13.
[20] Ms Collins became the first African American Prima Ballerina at the Metropolitan Opera in New York City in 1951.

[21] The Magic and the Commitment by Joyce Trisler. Dance Perspectives 31 ,Autumn , 1967 Page 56

dancers found the technique frustrating because their seemed to be no end. As soon as they had mastered the advanced studies, new ones would appear. " It was like starting all over again"[22], wrote Frank Eng, Horton's business manager and heir. Later, Horton trained dancers would be accepted into the companies of choreographers such as Martha Graham, Glen Tetley, Agnes de Mille, John Butler and Jerome Robbins. It appears Horton was successful in developing a spontaneous expressiveness in his dancers.

On November 3rd, 1939 the Horton Dance Group made its last major appearance at the Philharmonic Auditorium in Los Angeles. 1940 Marked the creation and presentation of *Sixteen to Twenty-Four* at Mills College in Oakland California. This work marked a shift again in Horton's work. The sections were titled: "Birthright;" "Problems- Men and Woman Without Work, Deferred Marriage, Threat of War"; and "Resolve". With this, Horton now began to look at the individual being affected by his environment. Previously his work dealt with the early ethnic period, through the social injustice and anti-fascist pieces, and the sweeping themes of American and Indian history. For the first time, Horton began to show concern for a generation plagued by war and the great depression. In 1942 Horton was invited by Universal International Studio's to choreograph his first major motion picture, *Moonlight in Havana*. In 1943 he was again contracted by the same studio for three other films, *Rhythm of the Islands*, *White Savage* and *Phantom of the Opera*. That same year Horton accepted the offer to bring his company to New York to open a lavish new nightclub, the Follies Bergère. 1946 marked the founding of Dance Theater located on 7566 Melrose Avenue in West Hollywood; it became the home of the dance company and the school. Dance Theater seemed to awaken an awe in the community, despite its humble facade, it inspired a young African American dancer by the name of Alvin Ailey, to sneak in and quietly observe a rehearsal from the back of the theater. Shortly after, Ailey enrolled in the school, and began his work with Horton who would become his mentor. In 1950 after his partnership dissolved with Dance Theater cofounders; William Bowne (Horton's Lover of 17 years), Lewitzky and her husband, Newell Reynolds, Horton continued running Dance

---

[22] "The Dance Theater of Lester Horton" By: Larry Warren, Frank Eng, Bella Lewitzky and Joyce Trisler
Dance Perspectives 31 ,Autumn , 1967 Page 56

Theater with the help of Frank Eng. The bitter and strained
relationship between himself and the latter had left Horton with an
uneasy and overwhelming sense of loss. He had always relied on their
continued relationship, and now most of the responsibility for
leadership of the company had fallen on him, and it was not in his
nature to take a firm hand when serious difficulties arose. Individuals
took sides, and Dance Theater was shaken to its core. Angry with
himself and at Ms. Lewitzky, he entered into a creative whirlwind. In
February 1950, a few days after the partnership was legally dissolved,
Horton announced a revival of *Salome*. Horton's choice for the lead
was a young, Carmen de Lavallade[22A]. After some adjustments to hide
her then technical shortcomings, and to highlight her lyricism and
feeling for drama, the updated version premiered April 7th, 1950. It
had been an exhausting and consuming period- from accounts, he
seemed to be getting very little sleep. He had reworked the twenty-
five-minute choreography, redid the costumes and sets, and dealt with
the leaving of two more dancers. The stress of Ms. Lewitzky's
departure, his breakup with Bowne, the long hours and the feeling
that he had to prove himself, finally led to his first major heart attack
early that summer. His illness had completely financially drained him.
Horton and Eng moved into the sewing room at the studio, saving the
cost of an apartment would help to make the next season possible.
1951 was the most financially difficult time that Dance Theater was to
know during Horton's lifetime, upon his recovery, and the advice of
the doctors to drink a little wine to calm his nerves Horton began
work on *Choreo'51*. It was a suite of "Fun Dances", and for the first
time, Horton was not working under the pressure to focus on social
commentary. The work was a colorful exploration of movement,
shapes, sounds and textures. This work gave him an opportunity to
renew his rich sense of theatricality. The program opened with *Tropic
Trio* in which the young Alvin Ailey made his debut in the section
entitled, "Frevo". Another work on the program, *On The Upbeat*, was

---

[22A] De Lavallade was born March 6th, 1931. She was raised in Los Angeles, and joined
the Lester Horton Dance Group in 1949 and danced with the company from 1950-
1954. De Lavallade began studying ballet privately with Italian ballerina Carmelita
Maracci and later acting with Stella Adler. In 1954, De Lavallade made her Broadway
debut in *House of Flowers*, and that same year, Alvin Ailey, the founder of the Alvin Ailey
American Dance Center School, moved to New York City to partner with her in that
production.

divided into four parts; "Brushoff Blues", "Kathak", in the North Indian dance style, " Pwe Bop", a variation on Burmese dance; and "Chassidic", an energetic Jewish feast dance. James Truitte, a dancer in the cast recalls," When the curtain opened on Kathak you saw pink, yellow, orange, green, blue, purple, red, silver. With the special lavender light on the fabrics we had tie-dyed, it looked like flames. Before we moved, the audience was applauding".[22B] Critics found the suite, "Breathtakingly colorful", "Spirited," and " Spontaneous". Horton felt it was some of his best lighter works. Since the late 1930's his designs had enhanced the sexual attractiveness of his dancers. The woman were often bare-legged and dressed in long flowing dresses, confusing those who had long associated modern dance with shrouds, winter underwear or long jersey dresses. The men were bare-chested or wore open necked shirts with their pants tightly fitted. It was the 1970's look that made them so alluring and confident in their sexuality, there was even an acceptance of it, Homosexuality was not discussed, and it was just a fact of life. For the high brow audiences who felt that his work was becoming cheap and bilious, he created one of his finest works, *Another Touch of Klee*. With jazz music by Stan Kenton, the work was divided into four choreographic excursions that alternated between moods of satire, lyricism, and fickleness all enhanced by subtle, dreamlike lighting. The work seemed to project beyond the proscenium, it became an example of a total theater experience in which the building itself was an intricate part of the creative process. It had evocative images, using elements of lighting, colorful costumes, bubbles, ropes and giant balls that made the tiny theater an intangible, " Place of magic".

Horton started drinking more and more, and claimed it helped him work. In an effort to relieve the financial situation, Horton also accepted to choreograph two musicals, *Annie Get Your Gun* and *Girl Crazy* at the Greek Theater in Los Angeles. Another, more practical factor in the development of his repertory was again an attempt to create pieces which would provide paying work for his dancers. Learning from his painful previous experiences, Horton asked his Principal performers to sign contracts stating they would be available for concert and commercial work for a period of at least one year in exchange for free classes and training. In the last several years, many

---

[22B] Lester Horton: Modern Dance Pioneer. L. Warren. Op Cit Page 151

dancers had come to him for training, and after staying long enough
to qualify as professionals, had left at the first gainful offer of
employment. In an effort to keep two separate identities the concept
of both commercial (Lester Horton Dancers) and a concert (Dance
Theater Company) units were created. However after a few short
months, the groups both comprised the same dancers. The dancers
were paid union wages for commercial work that would be found for
them. Horton himself however never accepted any compensation for
either his Choreography or for his costly and time-consuming
costumes he created for the group. Most of the fee for Television or
nightclub work was equally divided amongst the dancers. 1951 also
saw the creation of *Medea*, a choreodrama created for the company's
performances at the Ojai Music Festival in California. Like the
choreography itself, the score by Audree Covington had a raw energy
but lacked fineness. Carmen de Lavallade remembered a nearly
impossible dance of madness while smoke rose around her. The work
was under rehearsed because it had been put together in a hurry, it
was somewhat pulled together by the excellent performances of
Carmen de Lavallade, James Truitte, Rene De Haven, Jack Dodds
and Vida Solomon. It was greatly received at the Ojai Festival, but
after a slight reworking for Dance Theater, Horton put the work to
rest at the end of the season. Perhaps because Horton was still hurt
by his own feelings of rejection, the work raged from start to finish
and Horton would not allow himself such excessive emotional
behavior in real life and this work was perhaps an outlet for his anger
and anguish. The piece was never revived again. Talks about tours to
Mexico and Paris had fallen through due to the escalating financial
strains.

1952 prompted Horton (who had avoided formally consolidating his
work for many years because he felt it was an ever-changing, ever-
evolving technique) to codify his technique in its then current form.
Perhaps prompted by his ill health, Horton together with company
members; Luisa Kreck, de Lavallade, Kenneth Bartmess and George
Allen set out to refine and set eight semesters of seventeen weeks of
lesson plans. [23]. Soon other company members were drawn in,
including teenager, Joyce Trisler[24] who also joined the company in

---

[23] The House on Melrose,. Dance Perspectives 31 Autumn, 1967 Page 35
[24] Ms Trisler joined the Julliard Dance Theater at the invitation of Doris Humphrey
after leaving the Horton Company in 1956. She founded her own company in 1975 and

this year. He worked by setting each exercise to counts and then assigning dancers to notate the movements as clearly as possible. The next work session, the dancers were to teach the exercises from the notes. When the results had been tested, they were recorded in notebooks. Horton's objective was a book, carefully illustrated with photos and tentatively titled, The Basis of Modern Dance. There was also an idea of producing a film, however the finances could not be raised and the project was never completed. The notes are now worthless for reconstruction purposes as too much was left to the memory of the recorders, and years later an attempt to interpret them was to no avail. This period was however of great value later in solidifying Horton's teaching techniques. In late February and early March of 1952 Horton presented a series of lecture demonstrations in which he presented the results of the re-codification of the technique. This was the first introduction of his, "Fortifications", " Deep Floor Vocabulary", "Dimensional Tonus", Torso Language", "Pelvic Actions", " Fall variations", "Aerial Vocabulary", "Hand-Foot-Face Vocabularies" and "Turn Motivations". It was simply a clarification of the work he had done with Lewitzky, but had injected and re-captured the energy of the primordial movement research from his choreographic ideas.

1952 also saw the creation of *Liberian Suite*, with music by Duke Ellington. Horton designed some of his most laudable costumes and sets for this production, and its colorful and energetic movement phrases saw an understated primitive elegance and outbursts of joyous movement. It was well received by the critics who singled out Carmen de Lavallade and James Truitte for their abilities. Ruth St. Denis visited Horton that year, and although impressed with what he had achieved with the center, she was less impressed with the performance she saw saying," Dance should be a matter of head, heart, and pelvis." "Too much of here", she said of Horton's choreography, pointing to her pelvis, If you know what I mean".[24A]

Together, Horton and Eng mounted several successful seasons and Horton's group was the first established, multi-racial dance group in the country, he resisted any claims that he split the dancers up into

---

died in 1979.

[24A] Alvin Ailey: A Life in Dance. J. Dunning. Da Capo Press (1998) Page 49

ethnic groups, and was a campaigner for all dancers[25]. Even his long time friend and teacher, Carmelita Maracci[25A], who consequently also trained Carmen de Lavallade, James Truitte and Alvin Ailey and, who often shared students with Horton, made it, clear that, dancers should not enroll in their classes if they were not prepared to train with black students. Horton had already come under fire in the 1940's and 1950's for being a communist sympathizer. It was a time when McCarthyism[25B] was born, and all were suspected of being anti-American if you voiced disdain for the system. Horton, who refused to attempt to clear his name, insisted that anyone who hired his company be prepared to work with the interracial group of which Dance Theater was comprised. Up to that date he had been refused many important and prestigious bookings in Los Angeles and Las Vegas because of the political climate surrounding race integration in the United States. Bella Lewitzky described Horton as being, " profoundly interested in minority people. There was a great rapport and never a feeling of condescension. He was an active member of these communities a very warm and open relationship existed between him and these groups. He knew the Negro community and was welcome in their homes."[25]

---

[25] Alvin Ailey: A Life in Dance- Jennifer Dunning. Page 48- Da Capo Press (1998)

[25A] Carmelita Maracci (July 17, 1908-July 26, 1987) was a groundbreaking concert dancer, choreographer, intellectual, and teacher who had a unique blend of artistry, fiery passion and social consciousness. Official biographies state that Miss Maracci was born in Montevideo, Uruguay, but according to her husband, Lee Freeson, Miss Maracci was born in Goldfield, Nevada. Her principal dance studies were in ballet, with Luigi Albertieri and Enrico Zanfretta, and Spanish dance, with Hyppolito Mora. After performing with a touring group directed by Alexis Kosloff, Miss Maracci began to experiment with choreography that was a blend of ballet and Spanish dance techniques.

[25B] McCarthyism is the politically motivated practice of making accusations of disloyalty, subversion, or treason without proper regard for evidence. The term specifically describes activities associated with the period in the United States known as the Second Red Scare, lasting roughly from the late 1940s to the late 1950s and characterized by heightened fears of Communist influence on American institutions and espionage by Soviet agents

[25] Dance Perspectives 31 Publications, Autumn 1967 . Interview with Bella Lewitzky, Page 65

[26] A Vision of Total Theater by Bella Lewitzky Dance Perspectives, Autumn 1967

Early in March 1953, *Choreo 53* had its premier at the Wilshire-Ebell
Theater, as another attempt to improve the finances of the company
and as a dress rehearsal for the New York debut. The program
included a revival of *The Beloved*, Horton's fifth and final revival of
Salome (now called Face of Violence), and the premier of *Dedications in
our Time*, which included a homage to Ruth St. Denis, Martha
Graham and Mary Wigman and a section entitled, "Memorial to
Hiroshima". To this point, Horton had never created a dramatic work
in which a male dancer was the central figure. In his dedication
called," To Federico Garcia Lorca" a work for dancer, James Truitte-
Horton was said to be crafting his self-portrait. Frank Eng described
it as creating his own epitaph. Another gem of American modern
dance was his dedication to, "Jose Clemente Orzco", with a reused
score by Kenneth Klaus, which he had created previously for
Soldadera. It was often characteristic of Horton to reuse a good score
more than once. This work has been preserved and performed most
recently in 1973, in a revival staged by James Truitte for the
Cincinnati Ballet Company.

Two weeks after the *Chore 53* premier had ended, Horton and his
dancers loaded sets, props and costumes into two station wagons, and
headed for New York City, arriving March 24th. During the four days
of preparation at the Kauffman Auditorium at the 92nd street YMCA
in New York City, it became apparent that advanced publicity for the
group had been less than adequate. The event was in competition
with a two-week festival being sponsored by the billion-dollar
foundation of B. de Rothschild, and would include Martha Graham,
Merce Cunningham, Doris Humphrey and Jose Limon on the
program. Eng tried hard to publicize, only 500 tickets had been sold
for the two performances combined. The financial losses to the
company put a further strain on Horton as did the fact that one of the
major critics on a New York paper failed to review him because he
had not performed in a Broadway theater. The company therefore did
not get what they so desperately needed, East Coast recognition.
Although reviews from New York critic Walter Terry were glowing,
the opening paragraph's of Dance Magazine critic, Doris Herings
was not very excepting. She was quoted in saying, " His dances
appeal to the eye more than to the heart", complaining at the lack of

Pg.49

integration of emotion and the physical and pictorial aesthetic. The only work which got her approval was the duet, "To Jose Clemente Orozco", in which she praised Carmen de Lavallade saying," Miss de Lavallade is a find; Tall, Lithe, seemingly lyric in attack, she is also capable of wide emotional range and sustained dramatic concentration. And like all Horton dancers, she performs with a devotion that admirably reflects the atmosphere in which she has been trained"[26]. The unsuccessful debut in New York was the beginning of the end for Horton. Perhaps the stress of sustaining the company and the responsibility he felt towards his dancers, he started drinking heavily and was reportedly rarely seen sober[27]. The "Y" performances led to an invitation from Ted Shawn for the company to perform at Jacob's Pillow[27] in 1953, that following summer. Horton's importance and creativity as a choreographer and teacher was spreading and due to the successful appearance the company would be invited back to the Pillow the following year.

After returning to Los Angles, Eng became alarmed at how ill Horton had gotten, and decided that regardless of their finances, they could no longer live in the studio. After Horton's 19th film commission, *South Sea Woman* (1953), Eng and Horton moved into a small house in the Hollywood Hills. Eng managed to use the positive publicity from Jacob's Pillow and from the New York Performances to publicize another run of Choreo 53 which led to engagements at the then famous, Ciro's Night Club In Las Vegas, which was ready to accept a multi racial dance company. This set the stage for bookings with other organizations open to including mixed race companies. Until this time, offers to book the group had stipulated that Horton send only Black, White or Oriental contingents, separately, not combining them, he refused. Horton was busy again with long days, now apparently carrying a can of beer with him in the studio. On November 1st, due to the success of their run, Ciro's opted for another two-week extension of the company. The next day, November 2, 1953, the 47 year old Horton died of a heart attack in his home on

---

[26A] Lester Horton: Modern Dance Pioneer, L Warren. Op Cit. Page 185

[27] Located in the Becket, Massachusetts and founded by Ted Shawn in 1930. It is the longest running dance festival in the United States currently celebrating its 77th year.

Mullholand Drive.

A few days after his death, the American theater critic John Martin who failed to attend the companies New York debut and whom Horton revered and so badly wanted recognition from, wrote in the New York Times, "the death of Lester Horton of a heart attack last week comes as a great shock to those of us who took for granted that he would always be at work on the West Coast, supplying creative activity and energy and living support to the dance at the other edge of the country. Certainly he has been a tower of strength to the modern dance for 20 years, and his mark has been put indelibly upon it".[28]

Lester Horton's flair for theatricality, creative design and sensitivity for musicality gave us many fine choreographic works, including, *The Beloved* (1948), *Salome*[29] (1934), *Dedications In Our Time* (1953), *Liberian Suite* (1952), *A Touch of Klee and Delightful 2* (1949), and *Medea* (1951) to name a few. He had left his mark in film choreography, and was responsible for the dance sequences in 19 major motion pictures. Frank Eng succeeded in keeping the doors of Dance Theater open for seven years after Horton's death. During this period, Alvin Ailey began to make an unswerving impression while building his company, the Alvin Ailey Dance Theater Company. In the 1960's Carmen de Lavallade and James Truitte, both ex- Horton company members and students were featured in Ailey's company and were included in tours to Australia, South East Asia and the United States. Although few of Horton's works are still performed, ballets like The Beloved can still be seen in the repertories of companies like the Alvin Ailey American Dance Theater. During his lifetime, Horton's work had never been seen outside the United States. In the 1960's, Alvin Ailey was responsible for presenting two Horton masterworks, *The Beloved* and *Dedication to Jose Clemente Orozco* in Europe and Asia and which were highly acclaimed by audiences and critics alike.

In my discussion with Carmen de Lavallade[30] (teacher,

---

[28] Lester Horton, Modern Dance Pioneer. L Warren Op. cit.

[29] On the fourth production of Salome in 1948, Horton wrote his own score for percussion and human voice.

[30] Ms de Lavallade made her debut with the Lester Horton Dance Group in 1950 in the

choreographer, Broadway and film star) during a Horton Pedagogic seminar[31], she recalled that, "Lester preferred people and bodies who had to work harder, it became about the emotional conquest". She remembers there being much discussion and work in rehearsals, "this taught us stage decorum". Ms De Lavellade believes as do many of the original company members and teachers that the technique is evolving. " If Lester were alive today, with all this Hip Hop and Pop and Lock, who is to say it would not become part of the technique", says Ms De Lavellade. "Everyone is made differently, that is what he believed, and that is what we all know. Lester said that the movement should come out of your body, not be pasted onto you, it then became your work and your responsibility, there was no competition, only with yourself." During her acceptance speech for her 1967 Dance Magazine Award in New York City, Ms. de Lavallade said, " Long ago, Lester Horton told me that in years to come dancers would have to encompass all areas of the theater…and I think he was right. I would like to tell young people that this was good advice." Bella Lewitzky said of Horton," He (Horton) Painted dances more than he choreographed them. More emphasis was put on the telling of a story or the creation of a visual effect than on actual choreographic development".[32] In an article Horton wrote for periodical, Educational Dance he says, " Choreography should be approached in a richer environment. The modern dance has discovered its inherent theater and the implications are being realized on every hand-handsome wardrobe, more varied accompaniment, the spoken word, immediate contemporary meanings, and scenic investiture. The choreography of a dynamic dance cannot remain unchanging. It grows yearly more lucid, more versatile, more compelling. Instruction in Choreography should reflect the tendency of current works. It should find the student in a three dimensional environment, rich with sculptural masses, employing color and light in a significant way, utilizing the effectiveness of costume to enrich movement and meaning. Above all, the dance should be carefully and fully documented. That is the important thing, the factor which changes

---

title role of "Salome" She was 18.

[31] Interview given at the annual Horton pedagogic workshop held at the Ailey Studios, NYC July 2007

[32] Dance Perspective 31,Autumn1967 article. Page 59

choreography from improvisation to composition, which raises a variation to the level of a development".[33]

Horton's focus on creating a total theater experience established the groundwork for today's Dance Theater genre as refined by choreographers like the late Pina Bausch, Suzanne Linke, Anna Teresa de Keersmaeker, Robin Orlin[34] and many others. Horton's dancers were thrust into all aspects of the production, from sewing the costumes, designing and building the sets and creating the music and through his guidance Horton, was responsible for educating and maturing not only technicians, but also artists and performers. Lester Horton not only remains a dancer, teacher, choreographer and director, but most importantly- an overlooked inspiration for a generation of dancers.

---

[33] Educational Dance Vol 3. No. 3 By Lester Horton. August-September 1940

[34] German born, Linke is an ex-Baush company member, South African born Orlin is now based in Berlin.

CHAPTER 2
UNDERSTANDING THE TECHNIQUE

When considering Horton's technique one must bear in mind that in the beginning stages of its development, he had little or no outside stimulation or knowledge on the building or formation of a technique for the design of a dancer. The technique was not perfect. Without proper instruction, dancers could over-stretch, and some exercises were unnecessarily tough on the knees. His choreographic inspirations and ideas came from his experience with the traditional dances of the American Indian cultures. The long combinations in ethnic movement provided his dancers with a concise vocabulary of gesture and style. His interest in these primitive dances and practices laid the foundation for the architecture and design of his training vocabulary. Terry Maguire of the New York Reviewer stated in spring 1977," Horton is famous for producing dancers with long, lean, thigh muscles and flexible but strong lower backs"[14]. One could wonder if this phenomenon was deliberate on Horton's part, certainly he became more thoughtful of the dancers body as his experience with teaching increased.

All classes were taught using anatomical terms to describe the parts involved. Horton was insistent that his teachers were required to use the proper names. He began to place emphasis on breath and transitions, and perhaps with or without the influence of Humphrey and Limón, his technique began to develop with the use of a carefully designed flow. There was no vagueness in the way it was taught. The distinction between spacial planes was almost ignored. Movements were done on the floor and standing, but the floor work often included transitions to a standing position or to leaps into the air. His elevation studies also included falls. The bulk of his technique was designed to give dancers great facility in space. His expectations of endurance, flexibility and strength for his students and company members however, did not diminish, creating a technique embodied with dynamics, musicality, artistry and technical virtuosity.

The basic technique as codified and collected by Marjorie B. Perces, Ana Marie Forsythe and Cheryl Bell and published in a textbook form[15], lays the technique out as a simple and cohesive teaching formula. Many variations, additions and developments have been formed over the years by such master teachers as Milton Myers, former principal dancer with the Alvin Ailey American Dance

---

[14] "The Dance Theater of Lester Horton"By: Larry Warren, Frank Eng, Bella Lewitzky and Joyce Trisler .Dance Perspectives 31Autumn , 1967 Page 13

[15] Dance Horizons/Princeton Book Company (1992) Princeton, NJ USA

Theater and ex-Artistic Director of the now disbanded, Joyce Trisler Dance Company, and Ana Marie Forsythe, chair of the Horton Department at the Alvin Ailey School. These Horton veterans have kept the technique alive and constantly growing with the demands of existing and newly forming choreographers and directors. Considering that Horton's own choreography is no longer in wide circulation except by very few companies like that of the Alvin Ailey American Dance Theater, the creation of a codified research manual can provide dance students and teachers with a glimpse of the hard work which went into it's development as well as a first hand performance of some of his choreographic vocabulary. Many of the worlds' major modern training techniques such as Graham, Limón and Cunningham have shied away from the printing of a cohesive technique for fear of limiting its further development. It seems however necessary, at-least from a historical point of view, to have the original foundation of the technique published and preserved. Teacher and ex-Horton company member, Bella Lewitzky who, in her desire to give the technique a more formal and clarified shape, may well have prompted Horton to design a structure, complete with counts and musical phrasing. This was despite his fear that formality may curb the students spontaneity. In my experience as a professional touring dancer and teacher of the modern techniques, I have found it necessary to have a plan, but to be prepared to alter it depending on student's levels, studio space, and of course physical limitations of the dancers. Teaching does however become easier when a basic framework exists. The importance of having a codified text for dancers is invaluable in providing a source for reevaluation, structured training and a connection to a history of dance.

The Basic structure as laid out by The Dance Technique of Lester Horton divides it into roughly thirteen sections, which included; The Warm-up, Swings, Studies (namely Fortifications and Preludes), *Descents and Ascents, Stretches and Strengtheners, Falls, Turns, Isolations, Progressions* and finally, *Elevations*. These were derived primarily from Horton's experiences and work with the idea of four basic elements, which began with *Projections*.

Projections deal with specific qualities drawn from varied and dramatic sources. Projections can also refer to the idea of focus within the exercises. Horton's understanding of primitive movement captured the essence of Projections, which culturally were spiritual in nature, and are a driving force in the development of the technique as a performance tool.

With reference to Primitive movement, Horton felt that basic communication between humans could be physical, and achieved through running, walking, leaping, jumping, gliding and skipping, this led to the introduction of the idea of *Locomotions*, which were designed around the basic locomotive actions and which became the basis of the techniques theatricality and adroitness. Horton placed a great deal of importance on the experience of the student, and the basic material he provided in his classes contributed to *Improvisations* within the technique. These improvisations led to another section, *Developments*. Often a class could focus on a single movement and the development of this action into variations such as the signature Lateral " T" shape that evolves into front T, Back T, and Lateral T turns, Lateral T Jump etc. etc.

Fortifications

Consisting of 17 Codified combinations of steps to ensure structural protection and the utmost body efficiency, Fortifications form the bulk of the technique and are further subdivided according to the physical demands placed on the body. Fortifications focus primarily on;

a) Developing Stretch as in Fortification no. 1 for the Calf muscle and Hamstring muscle and Fortification no. 9 also known as the "Split Stretch";

b) Resiliency, as in Fortification no. 4 (Lunge study) and Fortification no. 6 (Abdominal Study). Fortification no. 8 (Hinge Study) and no.2. (Plié Study)

c) The Hinge and Plié studies respectively deal with the Range and Stretch of the movement.

d) Fortifications also specify Precision, Endurance, and Postural Alignment (all the basic studies are designed with this in mind).

e) Dynamic Stress as in Fortification no. 10 which incorporates the Front Fall and Fortification no. 11 (Basic Rise and fall) and,

d) Balance, which is quite prevalent in the technique and consists of the Elementary Balance study, Table Balance, 'T' Balance studies and the Coccyx Balance Studies.

Isolations

Isolations consist of: foot, hip, shoulder, head and torso isolations, and strengtheners[15a]. Later on, subsequent teachers, drawing from the then popular jazz choreography of Jack Cole[16]- whose teaching and style went on to influence the work of film and Broadway choreographer, Matt Mattox -added a series of Co ordinations and exercises as an addendum. These variations help to develop hand/eye coordination, hip and rib isolation, and head and hand opposition and can form part of the technique's dynamic vocabulary. Co ordinations can also be found in Fortifications no. 14,15,16. The use of all spatial planes and levels of movement creates a variety of physical challenges for the dancer. The majority of the isolations have a percussive quality. Bella Lewitzky has said, " Lester's technique was spatial in its emphasis, so it tended to reach outside the body. Our entire vocabulary in those days was fashioned out of exploration on the part of the company. Then Lester would draw from what we had done, guiding us towards the things he felt were significant and welding them into technical studies. "[17]. According to Joyce Trisler's interview for the Dance Perspectives publication in the autumn of 1967, " All aspects of tempo, movement range, rhythmical patterns and dynamic accents are explored". This was certainly apparent in Horton's classes where according to accounts; dancers often feared they would not survive one of his 2-hour sessions. Ms. Lewitzky goes further in calling the Horton Style an " Architectural Technique"[17a], using the elements of joint mobility and developing; throwing, flinging, swinging, casting and off balance movements to create a brilliant accretion of music, space, breath and dynamics.

The use of a rounding and arching spine by Horton was similar to the investigation of Martha Graham's contraction and release theory, all things flowed from the basic reaction of the breath, the contraction and release on exhalation and inhalation. Although his interaction with this modern dance pioneer was minimal, it seems only a natural course for him to investigate, no doubt in one of his choreographic sessions. His investigations led him to test the capacity of the body to

---

[15a] The Dance Technique of Lester Horton , page 182-186

[16] Jack Cole (1911-1974) American Dancer and Choreographer became known as the father of Modern Theatrical jazz. Danced with the Denishawn Dance Company as well as Doris Humphrey and Charles Weidman before persuing more commercial dance styles.

[17] A Vision of Total Theater by Bella Lewitzky Dance Perspectives, Autumn 1967 Pg. 48

[17a] A Vision of Total Theater by Bella Lewitzky Dance Perspectives, Autumn 1967 Pg. 48

move in extremes. His questioning led him to define the torso as being the origin of all motion; this was not dissimilar to the Graham and Humphrey/Weidman teachings. Horton also felt that other movement impulses came from the shoulder, sternum, diaphragm and pelvic region. This exploration could also have been what became known as his Dimensional Tonus or Yawn Stretch, which was many years in the making, and has all of these characteristics. James Truitte who worked closely with Horton explains, " The Horton Technique explores every part of the body, and works from the joint out. It is a logical exploration of the anatomy- nobody can put a label or stamp on you as to your technical background. This is one of the great identifying features of Lester's technique"[18].

Preludes

The next categories within this exploration are short phrases of movement that are designed to stimulate and tone the psychophysical instrument for a specific, disciplined action. There are 6 documented Preludes[19], all of these were dictated primarily by musicality which played an important role in Horton's choreographic work, often employing the use of large percussive scores played by the dancers themselves. His sensitivity to musical nuances gave rise to a deeper understanding of phrasing and dynamic texture.

Rhythms composed of musical dance patterns involved the student in common audible signatures of various cultures of the world. Horton was fully aware of the differences between rhythms of work and play found within these ancient, traditional cultures. His first choreographic work, *The Song of Hiawatha*[20] most clearly demonstrated his love for musical and rhythmic consequence leading to emotional manifestations. Preludes developed out of his search for more connection between movement and musicality.

Studies

Studies, as in the Fortifications, consist of approximately seventeen documented movement investigations. Many of these include variations and developments depending on student level and teacher creativity. These were further defined as consisting of Balance Studies that could be taught stationary or as progressions across the

---

[18] Excerpt from tape recorded interview of Truitte with Larry Warren in New York City, June 3, 1973- Liberary of Congress (RYE 7487)
[19] Dance Horizons/Princeton Book Company (1992) Princeton, NJ USA
[20] Premiering in 1928, this Horton work was based on the poem by Henry Wodsworth Longfellow.

floor, and began with the Elementary Balance Study[19a]. This is followed by the Table Balance Study, which progressed with the addition of plié, releve, leg extensions with variations as well as the Table Balance with Flat Back extension and promenade.

"T" Balance Studies which form one of the signature designs of the Technique, evolved from the simple letter 'T' shape of the body to a development of the shape to the front the back and with added Promenade, side fall and jump.

The creation of the Coccyx Balance Studies added another spatial level. Not only does Coccyx balance focus on abdominal and lower back strength, but through its advancements, allows for movement in the medium and lower physical planes. The Coccyx Balance makes use of additional elements of the technique such as Pivotal Decent and Accent, Front Recovery and the Pieta position, also known as Fortification no. 6, and which gets it's sculptural inspiration from Michelangelo's statue, the Pieta now found inside St Peters in Rome.

The Figure 4 study inspired by the design of the number four which is created by placing the ankle of one leg above the knee of the other in a standing position this can be done with either a bent or straight standing leg. This study has four sections with 5 transitions. All the studies can be taught in phases, or separate phrases before linking them together.

Prelude Studies consist of approximately 6 codified preludes although it is believed that some other documented ones exist, which could be merely a myth. Probably the most rhythmical and dynamic of the studies is the Percussive Stroke Study[19b] .This study is divided into five phrases with individual preparations for each phrase to facilitate teaching them separately and over time. It is recommended that many of these studies be taught over a period so as to allow for the appropriate detail in shape, timing and execution.

Another performance study is The Deep Floor Vocabulary[19c]. It consists of transitions that can be further divided into six sections and taught in separate phrases. It is fundamentally a control and a moving stretch study that uses the ideas of the descending slides, Triangle position and basic floor positions.

[19a] The Dance Technique of Lester Horton. Page 78-79
[19b] The Dance Technique of Lester Horton. Page 108-113
[19c] The Dance Technique of Lester Horton, Dance Horizons/Princeton Book Company (1992) Princeton, NJ USA. Page 113-123

Dimensional Tonus[19d], or the Yawn Stretch, is a carefully designed, fluid and lengthening composition designed to recreate an opening sensation in the body. It was the first study Horton created. This external action and its internal reactions leave the body stretched, while making provisions for isolations, dynamic twists, hip lifts and finger curls.

Horton's emphasis on core strength, as well as his focus on the hamstring and thigh muscles (Quadratus Femoris) led him to develop what became known as the Hinge Studies[19e] which Consist of 6 documented studies, each with variations and additions allowing them to build in sequencing and difficulty. The preparations for many of the exercises display the thought that was placed into their construction, allowing the student of dance to experience the correct sensations, initiations and shapes for these studies. Studies can be taught in increments and were designed not only for physical stamina, but for mental focus and performance confidence.

A prime example of a performance enhancing study is the Torso Language[19f] which, references a non-verbal vocabulary for the body, and particularly the torso, a factor which became increasingly important in the Horton technique. This study could have been inspired by Lester's work with Michio Ito. This composition encompasses the use of direction, dynamic execution as well as focus and these are all important developmental tools in the creation of professional dancers. One characteristic which can been seen in his dramatic works, is that his movement seemed to have its roots in gesture, not to say that it was pantomime, but rather that the movements expressed the dramatic idea behind it very clearly. In some of his works, like *The Beloved*, can be performed without the dramatic projection and still be absolutely clear in the relationship between the characters.

The use of space was vital to Horton, not only the side and front spaces, but the above and below regions. Similar to Graham's idea of the spiral, Horton created a series of studies known as Descents and Ascents[19g]. These pivoting combinations allowed for the strengthening of the inner thighs, the lower abdominals, lower back, ankles and even the connection of the feet on the floor. Many of the studies laid reference to shapes from previous preludes and studies this again is an indication of the steady and thoughtful development of the

---

[19d] The Dance Technique of Lester Horton page 123-129.
[19e] The Dance Technique of Lester Horton page 129-134
[19f] The Dance technique of Lester Horton page 134-135
[19g] The Dance technique of Lester Horton page 136-141

technique. Examples are the Figure 4 descent, Hinge Descent and Ascent, sliding Descent and the Pivotal Descents and Ascents.

Considering that the Horton technique in its pure form can be quite extreme on the body, the correct teaching and the knowledge of one's own physical limitations and goals are required. It is essentially designed to create dancers in the shortest amount of time and to correct physical faults. Horton became more aware for the need of balance within the technique, most probably through his association with Bella Lewitzky, and her influence on the clarity and need for purpose in each exercise. This detail can be seen also in the phase of the technique known as Stretches and Strengtheners[20a]. It is essential within the body to strive for equal strength as well as length and stretch. It seems that Horton was on to something that later on would be known as Active Isolated Stretching[21], a term most recently coined in sport physical therapy. AIS involves a continuous lengthening of the muscle, followed by a shortening, or contracting of the same isolated muscle while in a stretched position. It is believed that each time the muscle recovers from the contraction or shortening, the stretch that follows will be deeper and longer, allowing for the stretch to cover the entire length of that muscle from its origin to its insertion. This is believed to reduce fatigue and stress on the bulk or belly of the muscle. It is this continuous lengthening energy that plays such a large role in the principle of Horton's primarily linear technique.

Dancers bodies have certainly evolved last 10 years. Now days we primarily suffer from hip, knee, back and foot problems most commonly associated with Hyper Extension. Horton, in his desire to facilitate the construction of the dancer's body, saw fit to focus on these areas hoping to alleviate if not prevent these common physical phenomena. Examples of these will be discussed later on in this chapter. On that note it can be said that Horton still found it necessary to challenge the scope of the body as well as the gravitational forces present around it. His study of Falls[22], allowing for the illusion of collapse with a sensitive yet dynamic recovery encourages the dancer to think of the floor as an extension of space and thereby increasing the dancers sensitivity to it. Falls were designed to ensure the dancer, control and support of the body combined with the use of dynamics while playing with balance and

---

[20a] The Dance Technique of Lester Horton, Chapter 9, page 142-151
[21] The Active Isolated Stretching (AIS) method of muscle lengthening and fascial release is a type of Athletic Stretching Technique that provides effective, dynamic, facilitated stretching of major muscle groups, but more importantly, AIS provides functional and physiological restoration of superficial and deep fascial planes.

[22] The Dance Technique of Lester Horton, Chapter 10, page 152-163

off balance movements. His study of Falls included front falls, back falls, side falls, Back T falls, Lateral T Falls, front recovery, and rib cage recovery, all of which have preparations and additions, and once mastered could be used in creative ways to further challenge the idea of opposing energies within the realm of physical space. Falls were designed to bring the dancer closer to understanding the effect of gravity on the body. It is a necessity for the energy focus to be in opposition to this downward push, in order for it to sustain and control the speed or force with which it recovers on the floor. Within the concept of falls I teach the idea of suspension or "delaying the inevitable". This dynamic choice provides a further performance enhancing tool for the student.

Although he did not want his ideas to resemble balletic movement, his understanding of the basic needs of the student and the professional led him to adopt a basic Ballet class structure in which all aspects of movement would be addressed. The variations from the classical came in the different initiations the movements often had. His Study of Turns[22a] did not for example follow the conventional idea of spotting as taught in basic ballet classes. Instead, the actuation for these studies came from varying body parts, like the hips or elbows, and could be used as progressions across the floor. Another challenge to the student of dance is the fact that the torso in almost all of the turn combinations, is never erect. He always took a shape, and tried to continue the inherent idea until it evolved into something else, or merely an extension of the previous idea, as in his Table Turns, Stag turns, lateral T Turns, Hip Press Turns and Back T Turns all of which derived from basic studies.

Elevations

One exciting element of the technique is the creativity in the composition. Elevations, usually taught at the end of the class, are a source of freedom and energetic release for the dancer. Again, these often followed a broadening of an essential or basic shape, and were then jumped. What is remarkable is the emphasis on the musical and rhythmical element. Horton's Elevations distinguish and draw the awareness to whether the accent for a jump is on the up beat, or the down beat in the music as in his Single Foot Arch Springs[22b], where the accent and elevation is on the "and" count (1 and 2 and 3 and 4 etc.) and the landing and preparation on the count itself. This allows for the suspension of the jump to be up. The motive force for this

---

[22a] The Dance Technique of Lester Horton, Chapter 11, page 164-181
[22b] The Dance Technique of Lester Horton, Chapter 14, page 196-198

exercise comes not from the weight of the upper body leaning slightly forward as in Skips or Jetés, but instead it comes from the pushing of the pelvic girdle forward, thereby allowing the legs to straighten fully, in parallel, the feet to point directly down, and the pelvis to fall directly between the legs and inline with the spine. This clarification in rhythmical emphasis allows for more height in the body, and more strength in the legs. His Elevation Study No. 1[22c]describes leaps, springs, turning jumps, straight leg leaps and hops, and is a wonderful collection and investigation of the joy of elevation.

Propulsions

Propulsion is an important mechanism in movement, as is the transference of weight and both affect and influence the other. Horton's investigations into these basic joint reactions and the consequential muscle initiations, combined with his understanding of primitive movements prompted him to augment his principles into basic movement such as running, walking and crawling. From these basic motive forces he created movements with different impulses such as Elongated Runs with both legs straight, Accented Runs and Unaccented Runs as well as Knee Crawls. Swing became another important element within the technique. A Mexican-American choreographer by the name of José Limón[23] was playing with the concepts of suspension and released based movement on the East Coast. His influence came from Dancer and Choreographer Doris Humphrey[24], whose exploration of the effects of gravity on the body led to the idea of "fall and recovery", and Horton, still not having had exposure to Limón's work used the idea of joint range and swing to balance out his accented elements within the technique. It is widely believed that Joyce Trisler introduced the Release Swing into the class structure of the Horton technique giving it even more dynamic range and qualitative freedom. Leg swings, taught in parallel or turned out position, explore the idea of rhythm as well as provide a preparatory element for Kicks and Grand Batteménts. The idea is that a consistent timing is achieved by the swing dynamic and is therefore without an accent – the movement maintains a steady rhythm and has no dynamic change in timing or speed). They are also

---

[22c] The Dance Technique of Lester Horton, Chapter 14, page 198-200
[23] Limón moved from California to New York City in 1928 and enrolled in the Humphrey/Weidman School in 1929. After 10 years as an apprentice with the company, he formed is own company in 1946 with Humphrey as his Artistic Director and Co- Choreographer. Carla Maxwell is the current Director of the Limón Company.
[24] Dorris Batcheller Humphrey was born October 17, 1895. Considered a pioneer of American Modern Dance, her training at the Denishawn School of dance introduced her to Charles Weidman. After leaving Denishawn in 1928, she joined the faculties of the Bennington School of Dance (1934) and the Julliard School (1951).

an example of an Active Isolated Stretch, in as far as they allow for the continuous movement of energy and muscle stretch within the body, therefore the muscles are not left in a taut or extended position for too long, because of the release involved. It has a similar quality as a Pendulum in a Grandfather Clock, which keeps a consistent motion in the body and relies purely on gravity and weight. Horton played a lot with these ideas in the arms and torso as well. His Release Swing series focuses not only on stretching the hamstrings but strengthening and lengthening the back as well. Swings are also used as an initiation for Lateral T Turns, Swings and Lateral T jumps. The swing becomes an important factor in alleviating some of the muscular stresses on the body because of its emphasis on weight and the transference thereof.

Progressions[24a]

The blueprint behind the technique is the use of primitive movement and basic locomotive skills. Expanding these meant the technique developed into an organic cohesiveness between natural movement and artistic design. Horton was very much influenced by art as well, and combined his acquired observations into his movement such as his Egyptian Walks, inspired by the two dimensional drawings on ancient pottery and pyramids where the design paralleled that of the shape in the body. Progressions were shapes and designs that could travel across the floor making use of the applications of weight distribution and propulsion.

There are many shapes synonymous with the Horton style, when taught with the idea of continuous energy and length; they evolve into a fortifying training and performance tool.

[24a] The Dance Technique of Lester Horton, Chapter 13, page 187-191

Defining the shapes

An obvious visual trait of the Horton Technique is it's linear
appearance. This becomes clearer when comparing it to the other
modern dance techniques and more apparent if you consider its
creation was inspired by alignment, and the correction of faults and
weaknesses in the body. Like it's contemporaries, there are many
shapes and physical designs associated with its structure. Some are
more obvious than others, and many draw inspiration from a variety
of training techniques.

The linear idea as previously discussed is not only a design element
but also the expression and directional tool for the focus of energy. It
also makes the technique more accessible to students of dance as the
elongated lines often resemble basic ballet alignment. The Horton
technique is similar to say Cunningham Technique in the idea that the
energy moves consistently from the centre of the body, considered the
abdominal area, moving through the limbs, head, fingers and toes, in
a straight line, and never returns. The illusion is of a consistent stream
of energy flowing outward from the body creating a sense of length.
Structurally, it leaves the student with an undeviating, perfectly
aligned shape. The idea that your body is strongest when all the joints
are in one line, E.g. Hip joints over knee joints, knee joint directly
over ankle joint etc, allows for an organized anatomy and thus the
even and continuous flow of energy through those joints and muscles.
In contrast, the Graham Technique uses the idea of circular
movement, and the understanding that the energy flows from the
body in a circular direction, leaving the body, and then returning to
rejuvenate and deepen the shape like in a contraction of the spine.
The Limón understanding of energy flow involves a catch and release
of the energy. The momentum or gravitational element is used in this
technique to suspend the energy, and then expel and release it, so in
essence the body is without energy for a mere moment giving it the
fall and recovery element. If one considers these differences in energy
focus, it becomes easier to understand the arrangement of the body in
these techniques. Below there is a list of the basic Horton shapes,
which discern the technique and establish its foundational teaching
method.

The Flat Back

The first shape we encounter in a Horton class is the Flat Back Forward. With its focus on the hamstrings, and lower back, the Flat Back is a stretching and strengthening shape that calls for a lifting and forward sensation. The idea of the Active Isolated Stretch (AIS) comes into play here again in the sense of creating a continuous flow of energy from the bottom of the feet through the top of the head. Dancers often suffer from muscular strain, fatigue and stress, usually from either the over exertion of the muscles or the continuous use of the same muscle group, or area of the muscle. The Hamstring for example is located on the posterior side of the leg, consisting of the Biceps Femoris that originates in the pelvis, and attaches to the head of the Fibula and the Semitendinosus and the Semimembranosus tendons. The belly of the Hamstring, is the center portion consisting of the densest region of the muscle fibers, it is this section that very often suffers the most fatigue and stress. The aim in a Flat Back Forward stretch is to engage the entire expanse of the muscle in the action of its length, so therefore spreading the energy of that stretch over the whole muscle, from its' origin to the insertion. The hamstring muscle is used extensively in the Horton technique, so its efficient use is integral in the execution of the shapes. When teaching my students, I often use the idea of lifting up from the pelvic floor[25], before proceeding to hinge forward at the hips to create the flat back position. It is reversed on the way up and the sense of lengthening out of the crown of the head before stacking the hips on the legs again, and returning to the upright position. This idea not only allows for a continuous flow of energy through the backside of the body, but also brings the weight forward over the ball and toes of the feet, thereby spreading the involvement of the muscles to that of the Vastus Medialus of the inner thigh as well. I often teach a preparatory example where I ask the students to stand in a parallel second position facing the side, they are told to grip the under side of their Gluteus (Buttocks) muscles, closer to the origin of the Hamstring with their hands. As they begin their flat back, they are to pull up towards the ceiling with their hands, and continue this lifting of the Gluteal muscles for the duration of the Flat back to the 90° angle. The sensation is that of a long, and deep stretch, which is felt throughout the length of the hamstring. Visually, the dancers are forward in their legs, and not pulling back into the heels or hyperextension.[26]

---

[25] The region between the legs comprised of the Symphysis Pubis and Ischium bones.
[26] Hyperextension is a straightening movement that goes beyond the normal, healthy boundaries of the joint.

Figure 1. *The Flat Back*. Note the directional energy
flows to define length in the shape

The Primitive Squat position (Descending and Ascending)

Often taught following light knee bounces, and pliés, the Primitive
Squat position is executed in both parallel first and second positions
providing the Gastrocnemius or calf muscle an opportunity to
lengthen, as well as strengthen both the inner thighs, lower back and
lower abdominals. The legs are parallel; the arms are in forward
parallel in relationship to the floor with the palms facing inwards. The
legs are straight to begin. I have often given the image of sitting in a
chair, where the back should rest flat against a wall, as the knees
begin a deep plié. I encourage the dancers to go as low as they can
while always maintaining the pressure of the heels against the floor,
and the knee alignment completely over the tops of the feet. I
emphasize continuous motion so as not to sit in the shape at the
bottom of the plié. Therefore, the thighs are spared, and the
hamstrings have a chance to react and further facilitate and support
the stretch of the lower leg, as well as strengthen the hamstrings. For
the ascent to the starting shape, push down in the floor with the feet,
and contract the abdominals deeper while lengthening the knees and
returning to the standing position.

Figure 2. *Primitive Squat Descent*

Lateral Position

An equally important and consistently used shape in the Horton
technique is the lateral position. Structured to strengthen, and
stretch the *Latissimus Dorsi* and *External Oblique* muscles located on the
side of the body, this shape forms the foundation and basis for further
positions associated with the technique such as the Lateral - T, and
Side Hip Pulls, and studies such as the Percussive Stroke Study[27] and
Fortification Number 3, the Lateral Study[28]. The shape is taught
usually with the legs beginning in a wide natural second position,
with the feet turned out to appropriately compliment the turnout of
the dancer. The arms are straight and up over the head in a parallel
position with the palms facing each other. (Figure 3) The aim is to
achieve complete length and a constant energy flow from the bottom
of the feet, up through the inner thighs, through the lateral spine and
out the fingers and top of the head. The abdominal muscles are
engaged, and pulled inwards and upward thereby supporting the
lower back and creating more resistance for the stretch to occur.

To begin, there is a sideward movement of the pelvic girdle and hip,
this shift helps in creating space for the body to move laterally and

---

[27] The Dance Technique of Lester Horton,Page 118-113.
[28] The Dance Technique of Lester Horton, Page 59

remain in one consistent line, keeping the fingertips inline with the shoulders, and the shoulders inline with the hipbones. The head is kept erect on the spine and is thereby framed by the arms. The idea is that the entire shape moves simultaneously, (Figure 4) If one is to consider the concept that the body is strongest when all the joints are in one line i.e.; Shoulders placed over the hips, the hips falling directly over the knees, and the knees lined up directly over the ankles, one must consider then that this alignment of the joints and the bones helps to stabilize the body, and provide an oppositional structure from which the energy can rise up and out of the body. This is particularly true in the Lateral shape. When taught, it is necessary to inform the student that there is as much of a pressing down in the feet and *Scapula* (Shoulder Blades) as there is a lifting out of the fingertips and side hip. As the position is repeated on both sides, the stretch of the lateral muscles is increased. It is good to provide a mental image for the dancer, that they are executing the shape between two walls, one in front of the body and the other Posterior to the body. The hips are to remain facing forward and inline with one another, as are the shoulders, so as to allow for only the natural curve of the lower spine.

The lateral shape can be further subdivided into High and Low laterals where the foot is slightly off the floor and parallel, and the foot remaining on the floor is turned out and perpendicular to the front wall. The arms remain up over the head in parallel high position, and the hip remains facing forward and inline with the *Femur* (Thigh) bone, this forms the preparatory shape for the Lateral-T position and is an extension of the energy produced in a lateral shape. Variations of the Lateral shape are found throughout the technique and form part of its basic foundation.

Figure 3. *Natural second*   Figure 4. *Lateral Position*

with High parallel Arms

Figure 5. *Flat Back Right Side*

Figure 6. *The High Lateral*. Ensure the torso and outer arm is in direct
line with the outside of the working leg and that the
raised leg is in a parallel position and slightly forward.

It is important as a teacher to remind the student not to tense the
finger tips in the Lateral and Flat Back Side shapes, this will cut off
the flow of energy through the shape (Figure 5), also look out for the
maintenance of the turnout from the top of the legs in these shapes.
Ensure that in the High Lateral that the standing leg is turned out
and the working, or lifted leg is parallel, and forming a straight line
from the toes to the fingertips (Figure 6)

The Lateral-T

The *T- Shape* is the primary visual distinction found in the Horton
technique. Its variations are numerous and the shape can be used in a
promenade, turned, jumped and redirected to form not only a Lateral-
T, but also a Front and Back-T shapes where the consistent element
is the formation of a letter "T" shape with the body.

As previously discussed it is necessary to consistently emphasize the
importance for length and the attempt for a perpetual energy flow in
all directions. This is particularly vital in this shape, as it requires an
understanding of internal physical stabilization as well as a mental
image of an incessant growth in all the extremities originating from

the core or deep abdominal muscles. Balance and muscle control is the secondary focus of this shape.

The Lateral T begins much the same as the Lateral Shape, the only variation is the bearing of the weight on one leg as opposed to two, and the fact that the grounded or stabilizing leg is turned completely out, and the working or active leg is completely parallel. This opposition of the turn out not only helps to facilitate the hips being square in the position, but also plays a part in the alignment of the spine within the shape so that the dancer is able to control the turning and jumping executions and allow the shape to appear more linear. When taught, a reference should be made to the shape being merely an extension of the Lateral position. The side of the torso and gesture leg and the head with the arms in high lateral, are inclined to form a straight line to both the ceiling and the floor.

Variations of this shape include the *Back-T* with the front of the torso, the front of the gesture leg and face forming a straight parallel line facing the ceiling. The arms may be in high parallel or in second position. The standing or stabilizing leg may be bent or straight and is slightly turned out (See Figure 9). The heel of the standing leg may slightly rise to 1/4 relevé.

The *Front-T* consists of the torso, working leg and face forming a straight parallel line facing the floor with the gesture leg parallel and the standing leg slightly turned out, the arms remain in high parallel.

Figure 7A. *Lateral T Shape* (Previous Page) – Ensure the arms and legs are in one straight line and not higher than the other. Reiterate that there is a consistent flow of energy in both directions; the energy has to move at the same time, and at the same pace in order to achieve the balance of the Lateral T.

Figure 7B. *Lateral T with relevé* – When the correct balance is achieved, and the weight is placed on the front of the standing leg, it is possible to progress the Lateral T into relevé. It is necessary to push the energy down into the ball of the standing foot, as the position rises. The Lateral T Shape is Maintained, and not distorted as in Figure 7B where the relevé may cause the working leg to fall behind the torso, and the arms to raise slightly above a straight line.

Figure 8. *Low Lateral T* – This position is achieved by the continuation of the energy flow of the Lateral T in both directions. This is the reverse of the High Lateral (Figure 6). In this instance, the fingertips are reaching towards the floor, as the working leg is lengthening

away, and on an upward diagonal. Again look out for slight
deviations of the straight line

Figure 9. *The Back T*

The Standing Leg in the Back T can be straight or bent, ensure the
standing leg is as parallel as possible as in Figure 9. Be conscious that
the ribs are not protruding, the abdominals should be engaged and
supporting the lower back.

The Stag Position

The importance of the parallel position in the Horton technique is
integral as it provides the opposition to the turnout muscles of the leg,
and allows for the strengthening of the stabilizing muscles of the inner
thigh and outer hip. What makes the technique so accessible to
beginners and professionals alike is its clarity in shape and intention.
This is true in another defining shape of the technique: The Stag.

Usually introduced on the floor or after a series of parallel leg swings,
which assist the dancer in establishing stability in the hips and torso,
and assisting in the stretch of the thigh (Quadriceps Femorus
muscle), the Stag involves standing on one parallel leg with the other
lifted to the back, also parallel, with both hips facing the floor. The
lifted posterior leg is bent so that the toes face upwards, and the front
of the thigh maintains its parallel line. The torso is lifting up in

opposition to the leg, creating a stretch. The standing leg now can be bent or straight, depending on the study or teachers choice. The arms are straight, and connected to the back while the torso is twisting in opposition to the back leg. For example, if the right leg is raised to the back, then the left arm is spiraling back towards it, and the right arm is pointed forward. Both arms should be on a horizontal plane to the floor. This position, in keeping with the Horton tradition, can be progressed into jumps and turns and even introduced into floor work.

Figure 10. The Stage Position (In the figure above, the shoulders are too twisted, the aim is to have them be forward and inline with the hip bones.

The Table Position

An important developmental position within the Horton technique, the Table Position derives its name from the idea of a flat surface sustaining balance and shape. The Table position in all its variations has one basic element, that of a 90° position with the working or tabled leg, it can be executed with the leg forward or side in relationship to the hips.

While standing, one leg is lifted and bent at the knee at a 90° angle, where the top of the thigh is facing forward, and the lower leg and ankle are hidden from the front, the inner thigh of the working leg is parallel to the floor with the foot pointed. The standing leg is straight and slightly turned out to facilitate a comfortable and necessary displacement of the hip. The torso is aiming to be as upright as possible, again depending on the individual's physical range. I have found men have a harder time in this shape due to tighter hips. The arms in the table shape vary, but are usually either in parallel second with the palms facing down, or with one arm bent in front of the body in opposition to the leg that is in table, with the other arm remaining to the side. The head is forward.

This shape can be progressed by adding a flat back forward, relevé or executed as an outward or inward turn.

Figure 11. A) Front Table Position and B) Side Table Position

Ensure that the standing leg is completely turned out (Figure 11B), this should happen when the working or tabled leg is rotated from turnout into parallel table, both the legs are rotating, and again the idea of Parallel versus turned out leg is achieved. The lack of turnout of the standing leg would make the progression of the shape into a Lateral T difficult to maintain. Also the foot of the lifted leg of the dancer should not be seen.

Egyptian Walks

Many facets of art, music and folk stories sparked Lester Horton's creativity. A prime example of this can be found in his Egyptian position. Inspired by the two dimensional drawings and paintings on the walls and pottery of ancient Egypt, this parallel shape is another mark of the Horton Technique; it is also a further preparation for the parallel Stag shape.

Open Egyptian begins with both feet in parallel first, ankles are together and arms are at 90° with the elbows bent and the fingertips facing straight up, and not tensed. This should form a half "box shape" which frames the sides of the neck and head. The torso is facing straight ahead, as is the head itself. This shape, as in many Horton Progressions, develops into an Egyptian Walk. The feet remain in parallel first, when the right foot steps forward, it is placed down, in parallel and rolls through the Metatarsal, inline with parallel first. Simultaneously, the torso and arms, still in the Open Egyptian shape lengthen upwards from the pelvic floor and rotate towards the front leg. There is a clear oppositional twist between the front leg, and the torso rotating into that leg. It is imperative that the student is made aware of the vertical length as well as the horizontal twist, and that there is an awareness of the positioning of the elbows inline with the shoulders; the upper arms are perpendicular to the floor, and the forearms are parallel to the walls.

The benefits of this shape include a lengthening of the Erector Spinae muscles on either side of the Spine as well as a stretch and strengthening of the Lateral Oblique muscles. Further, as in a Yoga "twist", there is a school of thought that the pressure created in the organs and muscles during a twist, allows for freshly oxygenated and nutrient filled blood to re-enter those organs and muscles, once the twist is undone. The Egyptian arms are used widely in the technique in turns and often in Stag Jumps. Another variation is the Closed Egyptian. Here the legs are in a parallel second position, with the feet hip width apart, the torso and head are erect. The Triceps (Anterior muscles of the upper arm) are in front of the shoulders with the fingertips facing up, and the palms of the hands facing the dancer. The shape again frames the head and shoulders. Closed Egyptian is used in the Percussive Stroke Study and Figure 4 shape.

Figure 12. The Egyptian Walk   Figure 13. Closed Egyptian

In Figure 12, a common mistake is illustrated, both arms should maintain their parallel relationship with the front and back walls respectively; this can be achieved by pulling the shoulder blades down and into the back.

In Figure 13, it is important to note the tension in the Fingers and the hands; this should be addressed as it prevents the continuous idea of energy flow.

Coccyx Balance

Alvin Ailey[29], who used the shape in his 1960 Ballet, "Revelations[30]", made the Coccyx Balance shape famous. It forms the recurring motif in the male solo section entitled, " I want to be Ready". The Coccyx is a bone located on the inferior, or bottom of the Spine. It consists of roughly 5 Vertebra that are fused together and therefore have no mobility. The Coccyx is also where all the nerves of the Spine, end, making it a vital point for energy.

---

[29] Born in 1931 in Rogers, Texas- Ailey a student of Lester Horton, formed his own company, The Alvin Ailey American Dance Theater in 1958. He died of AIDS in 1989.
[30] Revelations premiered on January 31st 1960 at the Kaufman Auditorium at the 92nd Street YMCA. It is inspired by the Gospel Music of the African American culture.

The dancer begins lying on their back, on the floor. The legs are Parallel and the Ankles are together. The arms are on either side of the torso, with the palms facing the outside of the thigh. The head is on the spine, with the chin pulling slightly into the chest so as to continue the line of the back, the focus is up towards the ceiling. The Coccyx Balance shape is achieved by pulling the lower abdominals into the floor, and upwards towards the throat, at the same time. This abdominal lift, together with the sensation of pushing the lower spine into the floor gently raises the shoulders and the knees, (which are now bent) off the floor. The Knees and the Shoulders should be drawn towards each other, as the feet lift off the floor and the shins form a parallel line with the ceiling. The legs separate and allow for a small amount of space between the ankles and knees. The arms are raised slightly to be in line with the lower legs, the palms are now facing the outside of the Calve Muscle. This shape is achieved in three counts. The position is held for three counts as the energy is lengthened out the top of the head. The torso and pelvic floor are reaching in opposition away from one another. The shape is reversed all the way back to the start position, ensuring that the abdominals sustain their support of the spine by pulling inwards, and lifting upwards. The spine should follow its natural curve down to the floor in three counts.

Variations on the Coccyx Balance can be achieved by straightening the legs at the top of the Balance, lengthening the arms to high parallel and alternating between one straight and one bent leg.[31] This would later develop into Fortification number 6, or the Pieta as well as the Coccyx Transition or Coccyx Spin.[32]

---

[31] Refer to page 91-94 of The Dance Technique of Lester Horton.
[32] Refer to page 180 of The Dance Technique of Lester Horton

Figure 14. The Coccyx Balance Extended Legs

Figure 15. Coccyx Balance with

Strike Position

The Strike Position falls into the advanced portion of the technique and when taught, it is generally preceded by the Release Swings. These give the correct dynamic and impetus for what is to be called the 5/4 Swing[33]. The Strike position is achieved by driving the head, Torso and arms through a release swing, allowing the opposite leg to the side of the release, to extend up and off the floor. The gesture leg is bent with the arms reaching upward and parallel to the left thigh, the fingers are pointing to the ceiling. Both the arms are parallel with the palms facing in towards each other. Ideally the focus is towards the bottom shin of the standing leg, however in a 5/4 Swing, as the dancer is merely passing through this shape, the gaze often follows the path and swing of the arms as they recover through to a forward lunge.

---

[33] Refer to page 42 and 43 of The Dance Technique of Lester Horton.

Figure 16. The Strike Position. In a 5/4 Swing, the gaze may follow the swing of the arms so the torso is guided into the forward lunge recovery.

The Strike Position can also be progressed across the floor as a Strike Stretch.[34]

Lunges

An integral component to the technique is the idea of oppositional energies and stretch. As much as the technique relies on the flexibility of the Hamstrings and the length of the lower back, Horton also realized the necessity of counteracting and supporting these extreme body shapes by lengthening and strengthening the inner and outer thigh muscles as well. He developed a series of Forward and Side Lunges to achieve maximum stability in the pelvis, an increase of length in the Origin (area of muscle connection and origination- the Hamstring originates underneath the Buttocks), and the Insertion (where muscle attaches- the Hamstring inserts behind the knee).

[34] . Refer to page 148-149 of the Dance Technique of Lester Horton.

His Deep Forward Lunge Stretches[35] were created to stretch the hip joint, the insertion of the Achilles tendon into the Calf muscle, the adductors and the hamstring. The full series is usually given during the warm-up portion of the class, possibly after the Laterals. They offer the opportunity to dissect the parallel and turned out stretch of the legs. Fortification Number 4 (The Lunge Study) is carefully designed with the sense of alignment and the further exploration of deep and wide positions of the legs. Fortification Number 4 also includes a side lunge, which forms the basis for many sliding descents and quick floor recoveries. The Lunge, as in the practice of the warrior stance in Yoga, should have the sense of length and energy pulling in both directions, out of the crown of the head, and out the heal of the extended leg. Here again, the idea of a turned out front leg versus a parallel back leg is refined. Lunges give the body maximum range, while allowing it to rely more on gravity to assist in pushing the hips into the floor. This increases the depth and expansion between the limbs.

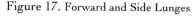

Figure 17. Forward and Side Lunges   Figure 18. Fortification Number 4- Forward   Lunge with Lateral, and Side Lunge with Flat back forward

---

[35] Refer to Page 150-151 of The Dance Technique of Lester Horton

Figure 19. The Cross Lunge. The Torso and head should remain in a straight line with the back leg. The arms can be are parallel to the back leg and with each other while the palms are facing inwards or with the right arm in Open Egyptian and the left arm in second (As in a Hip Twist Turn) The back foot is pronated.

The Hinge

The Hinge shape is an advanced sequence that includes a Quadriceps (thigh) extension, Gastrocnemius(calf) flexion, and combines hamstring, abdominal and lower back strength. The Hinge shape is usually introduced on the floor in a Horton class and the preparatory exercises are used to slowly and clearly introduce the extreme shape to the dancers body. The idea of the Hinge relies on the perfect alignment of the knee to the hipbones, as well as the hips to the shoulders. When learning a hinge decent while standing, the knees should be guided over the toes. This pulling of the knees down over the toes allows the heels of the feet to lift off the floor as the weight is taken into the thighs. The pelvis is in a straight line with the thighs, and is moving up on a diagonal, as the knees move down and forward over the toes. The Hamstrings at this stage form a completely supportive role, as do the calve muscles, which are supporting the ankles. It is important that the knees stay parallel to one another so as to provide the correct alignment of the Femur bones to the hip joint and protect the knees.

Horton utilized the hinge in many studies, and dedicated a whole series called Hinge Studies[36] to the refinement of this transitional and dynamic shape. The hinge shape is touched upon in Fortification Number 11 , *Basic Rise and Fall*[37] where it is used as a transition. In the *Spiral Fall*[38] the hinge is used as a mechanism for a spiral decent to the floor, using the support of the legs to spiral the body from a standing position to the floor.

Figure 20A. First Stage of Hinge

Figure 20B. Second Stage

Figure 20C. Third Stage of Hinge

Figure 20D. Hinge could progress into back slide

---

[36] Refer to Pages 129-134 of The Dance Technique of Lester Horton
[37] Refer to page 70-71 of The Dance Technique of Lester Horton
[38] Refer to page 156-159 of The Dance Technique of Lester Horton

The common areas to be aware of when teaching a Hinge, is to ensure the proper placement of the knees over the toes, in a parallel position. Also, as in Figure 20C, ensure that there is no arch in the lower back, this will place unnecessary pressure on the spine, ensure the muscles of the abdominal area are pulling in towards the spine, this should ease the pressure on the lower back.

The Hinge can also be utilized in the Back T, where the weight and execution is done on one leg, with the other leg lengthened and parallel to the floor and ceiling (Refer to Figure 9- but instead of a straight supported leg, the leg is bent with the principals of the Hinge applied).

A good preparatory shape for the Hinge is the Flat Back, Back Bend or Pelvic Press (Figure 27). This provides the foundation and clarity for the direction of the pelvis in the Hinge.

The Figure Four Position

The integrity found in the shapes of the Horton technique is a remarkable tool for training students. The terms and names used to describe positions and exercises are some of the most defining features of the technique. The Figure Four shape, created by placing the ankle of the one leg over, above and in front of the knee of the standing leg, thereby creating the number Four with the limbs. This shape again is refined in the Figure 4 Study[39]. This study is a good Iliotibial Band[40] stretch and also provides opening for the rotating muscles of the hip. Figure 4 can also be progressed into inward and outward turns.

[39] Refer to page 94-99 of The Dance Technique of Lester Horton
[40] The iliotibial tract is a superficial thickening of tissue on the outside of the thigh, extending from the outside of the pelvis, over the hip and knee, and inserting just below the knee.

Figure 21. The Figure Four

Horton and the Body

I have often compared the structure of the human body to that of an architectural creation. It is relatively simple in design but complex in its construction and, completely reliant on an understanding of the inner workings. When teaching Horton technique, I always try to emphasize the importance in the knowledge and self-awareness of the body. In my experience in teaching children; pre-professional and professional dancers, their experience of basic anatomy is quite varied. I am always amazed at how little dancers know about their own bodies. In essence, it is our knowledge of what we have that allows us to understand what we can achieve.

Although Lester Horton's own basic knowledge of anatomy was quite minimal when he started choreographing and teaching, his research and development of design combined with his own physical and functional compromises, led to the creation of a powerful training tool in the formulation of the dancer's body. When looking at the technique as a whole, it is clear that not only does the functionality of the technique evolve with the student's abilities, but there is also room for the individual body type to assimilate the principles and translate them personally.   Essentially he developed a technique that Bella

Lewitzky described as, "testing the capacity of the body to move in extremes"[41]. When experiencing these extremes it is still very clear that there is always a neutral position from which you initiate and to which you recover. This seems to provide the technique with a true sense of dynamic actuation that allows the body to explore its true capabilities and understand its limitations. The Horton Technique has often been described as a logical exploration of the anatomy, which in my opinion is quite interesting considering that dance, and the pressures and stresses placed on the body, are quite illogical.

In my own exploration of the technique, I have found its effects on the body to be quite intense. The physical changes are immediately noticeable, especially when training 3 or more times a week. I have found the lower Lumbar[42] region of the spine is reinforced and, the hamstrings are lengthened. The lateral muscles on the side of the torso become quite defined and lengthened. However, if taught with the wrong emphasis and without proper preparation, these areas can also be strained. It is incredible to note that the technique makes provisions for every part of the body. From the toes to the fingertips, or whether the focus is placed on the length of the head, or the pressure on the soles of the feet on the floor, the idea of the total body experience is wonderfully entertained in a ninety-minute class.

I tell dancers that if they can understand their technique mentally and without the aid of gesture or movement, and, be able to explain in detail what is physically occurring and where the initiation is, then they will understand and be more efficient in executing it physically. It is important in any technique, but specifically the Horton technique that the dancer understands why; why the standing heel is turned out in the Lateral T position, why there is a hip displacement in a Lateral, and why there should be consistency in muscular length. The why helps the dancers understand the how, and in turn the possibilities of its craftsmanship.

A wonderful example in the technique of a total body experience is the Dimensional Tonus, or "Yawn Stretch", which activates and stimulates every aspect of the dancer's anatomy. It deals with all the physical planes, all the joints, and length in all the major muscle groups. Considering that the physical demands placed on dancer's bodies have changed quite dramatically since the advancement of the modern techniques, it is amazing that Horton's understanding has translated so well into the bodies of today. The use of the technique in

---

[41] "A Vision of Total Theater" by Bella Lewitzky. Dance Perspectives 31 (1967) Page 48
[42] The lumbar vertebrae are the largest segments of the movable part of the vertebral column. They are designated L1-L5 starting at the top. Located in the lower back.

the teaching of professional company class is exceptional. The aspects, of alignment, mobility, cardiovascular exertion, muscular strength and stretch are all covered. It seems easier with the professional as they seem to have a clearer understanding of their bodies. Professionals are use to adapting choreography and its nuances for there own bodies, but then again the main point in the technique of performance is finding your own voice and discovering what aspects suite and enhance your performance. I have found however that is becomes necessary when working with professional dancers in a company class setting, that they respond better to the technique physically when it is introduced after a initial warm up, perhaps Yoga or light cardio vascular activities.

In my own experience, having solid ballet training, but having supplemented that with Graham, Limon, Cunningham and more exclusively Horton, I have an understanding of its structure and therefore its strengths, which has made me more able to adapt to the physical challenges of other techniques and choreographers.

When discussing the benefits of the technique on the body, one must also be aware of the contrary effects. I have often noticed the number of Hamstring injuries in dancers, particularly in the lower levels, before they have an understanding of how much physical force they need to execute or achieve a position. This is a difficult aspect to teach as it has a lot to do with the quality of the movement, rather than the quantity, this also comes with experience. I do feel however in the Horton technique that the dancer is quickly made aware of how much to push their bodies. Especially when dealing with muscle groups that are not readily engaged, such as the lateral torso muscles.

In a comparison study by Ruth L. Solomon[43] (BA) and Lyle J. Micheli[44] (MD) held in 1986[45] in the Physicians and Sports Medicine Volume 8 of August 1986, the common weaknesses and injury prone areas among the major modern dance techniques were paralleled. 164 students were questioned of them 127 were women and 37 were men. 10.8% complained of knee injuries in the Horton technique, compared to 25% who studied in the Graham Technique. This could be attributed to the emphasis placed on the engagement of the thigh muscles when standing. This involves lengthening the Quadriceps muscles up and keeping the kneecap supported. 21.6% complained of lower back injuries sustained with the training of Horton technique

---

[43] Professor Solomon was the Director of the dance theater program at the University of California in Santa Cruz. She is also the co-author of, "Preventing Dance Injuries".
[44] Dr. Micheli is a fellow of the American College of Sports Medicine.
[45] From the Aticle, Technique as a Consideration in Modern Dance Injuries, The Physician and Sports medicine Vol. 14. No. 8. August 1986. Page 85-86

compared to 16.7% in the Graham Technique. This could be caused by the continual use of the flat back without reiterating abdominal support. Foot and hip injuries seemed minimal when compared to the Cunningham and Limon techniques. It was found that the Horton technique engages the quadriceps muscles in a way that stretches and strengthens them, a process that is help full in preventing knee injuries. Similarly, the Graham technique uses the concept of continuous contraction and release that stretch and strengthen the abdominal and Iliopsoas muscles. This is almost like repetitive pelvic tilts which help to prevent lower back injuries. It seems necessary then to assume that a balance and an understanding of anatomical design and structure is integral in both the teacher and student approach to Horton. Finding the correct structure of a class is imperative not only to inspire the student, but also educate the body.

According to a 2004 Study by Shaw Bronner[46], (PT, MHS) of the International Association for Dance Medicine and Science[47] (IADMS) which concluded that, working in parallel without the assistance of a barre and working asymmetrically with one limb in parallel and the other turned out (which are all prevalent in the Horton Technique) caused ballet trained students with an otherwise deep understanding of alignment and stabilization to technically, "fall apart". Perhaps because the body is subjected to different stresses in Horton than it would be in ballet. In a survey conducted by the IADMS that same year, Horton teachers were asked to list the 5 most difficult movements or sequences for beginner students, there response included; "flat backs", "laterals", "pelvic press", "hinge position" and "table position". The common areas of stress in the body were the hamstrings and lower back.

In 2005, the same organization conducted a study on the Modification of the Horton Technique Class to minimize potential stressors[48]. Led by Dana-Hash Campbell[49], as well as Shaw Bronner (PT, MHS, EdM, and OCS) and Sheyi Ojofeitimi (MPT). In-order to effectively reduce the risk factors in the Horton technique; the dance educator must asses whether the Horton technique class is the student's first

[46] Ms Bronner is the in house Physical Therapist for the Alvin Ailey American Dance Theater. She is also affiliated with the Long Island University and is the Director of the Analysis of Dance and Movement Centre, located in New York City.
[47] Article and Proceedings for the 14th Annual Meeting of the IADMS. Edited by Ruth Solomon and John Solomon. Page 25-26
[48] Article and Proceedings of the 15th Annual meeting of the IADMS. Page 121-122
[49] Chair; Modern, Ballet, Dance Wellness department of Long Island Univrsity's Brooklyn Campus. She is an Associate Professor of Dance and Chair of the Dance Department. She has served as trainer, recruiter and rehearsal director since 1997 and was a principal dancer and company teacher with the Alvin Ailey American Dance Theater until 1995, when she retired to return to school.

lesson of the day and whether the modern dance student is a beginner. It was suggested for example that the flat backs and laterals be placed later in the class following a series of preparatory sequences. I have found it necessary to start the class with a series of flexion and extension exercises for the back such as arching and contracting. Gentle upper body circles have also been effective. I find introducing hip isolations and upper back curves assist in preparing for flat backs. I like to start the class off with gentle plies in all positions, primarily as a preparation for the hamstrings and hips before the spinal roll downs. I also find it grounds the dancers and brings their awareness to their centers. It is also suggested to place the leg swings before the laterals to better prepare the hamstrings and hips.

It is important to remind the dancer that the same core abdominal musculature that they practice in a ballet class, must be integrated in their Horton technique. It is also important to review with the dancer the neutral spine and pelvic alignment in changing postures, and reiterating the importance of not locking the knees (sitting back) into hyperextension, and thereby tilting the pelvis anteriorly.

The use of an energetic image of oppositional energy through the torso and head help the dancer to resist a posterior shift of the pelvis. The idea that the pelvis is always stacked on top of the legs helps the student to maintain an "active" neutral pelvis and possibly reduce the stress on the Hamstring and Quadriceps.

Dynamics also play a part in how the technique affects the body. If all the initiations are sharply executed, this again places a strain on the backs of the legs, particularly the area behind the knees, but if it is made clear that the Horton technique should have a lyrical quality, then often the dancers begin to adopt a more efficient approach. Lower back complaints, are almost always the case in dancers who have week abdominals. Although provisions are made within the technique for this weakness, by means of the Coccyx Balance Series[50], it is important that the dancer understands that the abdominals should always be pulled in, towards the spine, and up, towards the throat. It is important also to mention the connection of the Scapula[51] or shoulder blades, and how they should be pulled down away from the ears. The rib cage should be closed, (I use the image of a corset which limits forward and backward rib movement)

---

[50] The Dance Technique of Lester Horton. Page 91-94
[51] Also known as the shoulder blade, is the bone that connects the humerus (arm bone) with the clavicle (collar bone).

but, allowing space for the expansion of the chest sideward, the breathing then assists the body in expanding the back laterally rather than affecting the chest, this breathing technique differs from actors and is often employed by opera singers to achieve long sustained notes. This thoughtful breathing helps the dancer to maintain the stabilization of the core muscles and assists in supporting the spine. This is the sole purpose of the abdominal muscles in the body.

I have also observed that the thigh muscles may have a tendency to build, which again can be neutralized if emphasis is placed on length in the entire leg, and the full use of the inner thigh muscles to assist and support the idea of rotation, even in the parallel position. Shapes such as the Stag Position, Parallel leg swings and even the Deep Lunge Series, can help in the tightness and length of the quadriceps muscles. If we consider that the body was designed to have the weight and energy run through the midline of the body. This would explain the placement of the spine in the middle of the torso between the ribs and limbs, and also the placement of the head that maintains the heaviest portion of our bodies over the center of the torso. To have the student understand the functionality of this concept, as well as the importance of the use of the inner thigh as a supportive and collaborative muscle to the outer thigh, I encourage the dancer to place awareness and slightly more energy to the "pad of fat" located below the origin of the big toe. When in relevé, if slightly more weight is distributed to this point of the foot, the inner thigh is forced to engage, and the sense of a lifted pelvic floor can be more readily felt. This also prevents the weight being forced to the outside of the ankle, which, may cause weakness or injury and the encouragement of a pronated or sickle foot. I also encourage the dancers to keep their weight slightly forward during flat backs and laterals so as not to overwork in their Hyper Extension and contract the thigh muscles.

The ability of the body to learn and communicate is an incredible tool for the performer. It is important to be aware of the body's ability to compensate and readjust for weaknesses or difficulties in the technique. I have always believed that an educated body is an important part of a memorable career. If you are a teacher, you have a responsibility to your students, if you are a student; you have a responsibility to your body. The Horton technique is a wonderful tool in achieving these goals, allowing each aspect of the dancers body to be addressed and thereby re a firming the strengths and facing the weaknesses.

"Lester was a born teacher. He felt it was not enough to train the body. A technique class would include references to art, music, politics-anything that might relate to what he was doing at the moment. Imagery, however, was never a substitute for technique. You could think all the beautiful thoughts you wanted, but if the arms and legs weren't right where he wanted them, you might as well forget the whole thing[52]"   Joyce Trisler

---

[52] The Magic and Commitment- Dance perspectives 31 (1967). Page 64

CHAPTER 3
THE HORTON CLASS

What to expect:

My first experience with Horton was at the Alvin Ailey School in New York City in 1998. Having a background predominantly in Ballet, Jazz, Tap, Classical Greek dance, Graham Based modern, Flamenco and West African dance; I was immediately drawn to the Horton Technique's rhythmic, dynamic and powerful elements.

Since that first class, I have taken countless classes with masters in the technique such as Milton Myers and Ana Marie Forsythe and sat through lectures from ex Horton company members, such as Carmen de Lavallade[53] and taught and investigated as many aspects of dance technique and performance as I could, and still to this day, I get an eager exhilaration every-time I enter a Horton class. Whether it is the complex musical rhythms, the nuances of each body part, the physical and mental goals set with each Fortification or Prelude or Study, or just even the sense of accomplishment when I discover something new- The Horton class is a technical, sensual and dynamic vehicle for students and professionals alike.

As a teacher[54] I have found it an incredibly energetic technique to pass on to students. I often get caught up in the vibrancy and excitement of the students as they balance, turn, fall and sweat. In this chapter we will deal with the structure of a Horton class, how to train professional dancers, in a company class environment, as well as master class and workshop teaching. I will also discuss the benefits of the technique for students of modern and contemporary dance.

---

[53] My interview with Ms de Lavallade was held at the annual Horton pedagogy seminar at the Ailey school in New York City during the summer of 2007. This conference is open to international teachers who are interested in developing in the Horton Aesthetic. It is run by Ana Marie Forsythe.
[54] My career as a teacher began when I was a dancer with the Alvin Ailey Repertory Ensemble in 1998 although I have had experience of teaching Tap and Jazz classes in South Africa before that time.

Horton for students: the benefits of the technique for students of
Modern, Contemporary and Classical dance.

As a student, the dance class is much like a lesson in language. As in
any form of communication, there is a design that has to be followed
in order to most accurately portray ones emotions. This design would
include; grammar, punctuation and vocabulary as a mode of
expressions within the style. In dance, these take the guise of
dynamics, technique and expressiveness and, as a teacher, it is
important to create a safe, fun, and daring environment where the
dancer can investigate and assimilate as much of their language
vocabulary as possible.

 In any class, the warm up is an important preparation for the
student, but I have also found it necessary to encourage the student to
arrive earlier and gently stretch themselves in preparation for a the
class. The Horton technique was developed in California on the west
coast of the United States, a very warm and humid climate, perfect
for the musculature of a dancer. The technique was then taught
almost exclusively in New York City on the east coast, which has a
colder climate, especially in the winters. I have found this information
particularly important because there is a need for a longer warm-up
in a colder environment, particularly if it is their first class of the day.
For this reason, elements were later added to the warm-up, which did
not exist in the original class structure. The Roll Down for example is
an east coast addition but, during the techniques development, the
Flat Back would be the first exercise, the warm climate in L.A made
this easier on the dancers body.

The Horton technique provides beginner dancers, who have an
understanding of alignment and support from their center, with a
sense of accomplishment. This becomes noticeable because the
technical vocabulary builds and the shapes are accessible. For the
advanced dancers, the class offers an opportunity to develop
important dynamic, and musical tools as well as integrating
visualization and setting personal goals within a class.

The Warm Up.

The Horton warm up consists of a series of preparatory and focus
based exercises to bring awareness and clarity to the body and the

mind. The Warm up is comprised of what has become known as the "Basic 7", and include the Roll Down, Flat Back Series, Primitive Squat with bounces, Laterals, Release Swings, Leg Swings and the Deep Lunge. The student will experience all or most of these in the course of a class.

- The Roll Down is the basic preparation for the spine, hamstrings, knees and Achilles tendon and is counted in 4's and 2's. The roll down provides the body with a focused stretch and length of the spine and Hamstrings. The dancer is encouraged to allow the weight of the head to drop forward as the chin falls to the chest, the head continues to roll forward as the muscles of the spine articulate and the body bends forward at the hips this is the point when the Hamstrings become engaged and lengthened. It is then reversed, stacking the Vertebra back on top of one another until standing. The Abdominal Muscles are engaged through out, and it is helpful to remember that the Hamstring cannot obtain its full stretch until the lower back has released. Although this was a later addition, it has become integral in preparing the body to experience the technique. The Roll Down is usually followed by,

Figure 22. The Roll Down (The Roll Down positions are reversed to bring the body up to standing)

- The Flat Back Series which is counted in 3's, and is designed to stretch the back of the legs and strengthen the lower back while engaging the muscles of the arms and the upper back. The Flat Back series consist of a plain flat back, hinging at the hips, and allowing for optimum stretch of the back of the body. Flat back with arms, flat back with plié, flat back with relevé, a combination known as the Eleven threes', consisting of a set of eleven counts of three and the introduction of the low diagonal flat back. The Flat , Back, Back Bend or Pelvic Press is also introduced and serves as a preparation for the Hinge as well as for the placement of the head for Back T. The series ends off with a roll down into a flat back, which is repeated four times, and then the reverse which consists of a flat back into a release forward and a roll up, also repeated four times. It is important to note that because this is still a preparatory stage for the body, there is no accent in the flat back or roll down. The only accent is for the arms on the "and" count in the final two stages of the combination.

Figure 23. Flat back with Plié.   Figure 24. Flat back with
Low diagonal

Figure 25. Flat Back, Back Bend

- As a release and an opposition to the extreme movement of the flat back, The Primitive Squat[55] provides an opportunity to elongate and strengthen the inner thighs and Quadriceps as well as preparing and gently lubricating the knees. The parallel position is very important for Ballet trained dancers

---

[55] Refer to the photograph titled Figure 2 for the shape.

who are constantly externally rotating. The Primitive Squat introduces the control that is needed in the inner thigh and the lower Abdomen while on two legs. This creates the gentle stretch of the muscles located in the front of the leg and an opportunity to find a neutral spine and pelvis, which often can be distorted in a turned out position.

- The Lateral Stretch is an important part of a Horton Warm up. The Laterals provide the stretch and strength in the side body, lower spine and oblique abdominal muscles which are necessary for the execution of many Horton shapes such as the; Lateral T, Side Hip Pull and Side Fall. They are given with diminishing counts, and with variations that include; Lateral with Flat Back, Lateral with full Plié, Lateral with Horizontal Swing and Lateral with Release Swing[56].

- Laterals are usually followed by Release Swings which offer the student an opportunity to experience dynamic variation, physical attenuation as well as an increased stretch for the Hamstring muscles, Lateral body and the lower abdominal. The basic stance for a release swing also provides for ankle stabilization through its many variations[57].

- After the stationary warm-up sequences, Leg Swings are given as a preparatory exercise for the hips and a further release and lengthening of the Hamstring before the legs are employed for kicks or slow, controlled leg lifts. They are taught usually in parallel in the Horton technique for stretching the front of the thigh in preparation for the Stag position. I have often given them turned out which provides a slight release for the side hip, thigh and Buttock[58].

As a side note, it is important to make the student aware of the reasons for dynamic variations in the technique. I always believe that if a student understands the principals of an exercise in there minds then it will be absorbed much faster in there bodies. For example, understanding the basic difference between a leg swing

---

[56] Refer to page 35-36 of *The Dance Technique of Lester Horton*

[57] Refer to page 38-45 of The Dance Technique of Lester Horton.

[58] Refer to page 47-53 of the *Dance Technique of Lester Horton*

and a kick is often unknown to students of dance. It is important that they understand that the dynamic accent of a movement's execution, dictates the physical value.

Leg swings, as they are essentially a preparatory exercise, have no dynamic accent, again I use the image of a pendulum inside a grandfather clock. There is a consistent rhythm in the swing and the focus should be on regulating the height and weight of the leg being manipulated. The Grand Battement (Kick) , has an accent, whether up or down, and provides more height, and has a lighter but more dynamic rhythm.

- The Deep Lunge Series[59] is a Quadricep, Iliopsoas, Hamstring, Tensor Fasciae Latae and Lower Gluteal stretch. It is usually given half way through the warm up as another opportunity for stretch in the lower body. The Deep Lunge is executed with the front leg in turnout, and the back leg in parallel. In Horton, the use of one parallel versus one turned out leg is engaged a lot in the technique and is used to maximizing the turnout on that leg while the resistance is provided by pushing down into the ground.

Although the "Basic 7", form an integral part in the dancer's understanding of Horton's principals of linear placement, teachers often make use of variations depending on the level of the students, the goals of the class and the environment, which often play a large part in class structure.

Student goals or expectations in the case of a master class are very different to those in a conservatory environment. In the case of a single class, it is imperative that the basic principals and shapes of the Horton technique are given in the purest way. I have found then that the students leave the classroom educated in the style and aesthetic of a Horton modern class. In situations where I have had students for longer periods, or who may have had partial or extensive exposure to the technique, I can then be more creative in my structuring and variations within the Horton aesthetic.

---

[59] Refer to page 150-151 of the *Dance Technique of Lester Horton*

It is obviously more productive for a student to spend time in a particular technique to really begin to grasp the nuances and benefits. The linear quality, much in the way of classical ballet, is what makes the Horton technique so accessible for many students. Similar to Ballet, Horton can also be recognized as a, "shape orientated technique"[60]", as so defined by the Alexander method of physical classification. Horton provides both visual and physical land marks for the student, even the names of the exercises are clear in the focus and intention, of either the shape being achieved, the image created, or the dynamic quality being produced, these include, the Lateral T, which forms the capital letter T shape with the body, the Flat Back Series, or the Percussive Stroke[61] study which refers to the accented and dynamic quality present in this series.

Another engaging quality of the technique for students is their ability to track there own improvement and technical growth through the variations of the basic shapes and the studies. It is therefore possible to further inspire the student to continue to work on the refinement of the technique. The physical changes can be quite evident as well. Although, these largely depend on individual body type, the number of Horton classes taken, and what other dance or physical training the student is involved in, never the less, it can be an exiting and inspiring change that can be noticed throughout the progression of the training. In my body for example, I noticed more definition in the side torso, back, thighs and shoulders. I also felt more strength in both my upper and lower abdominal and lower back. Female dancers can benefit from the lower back and abdominal strength as well as the toning of the thighs and arms.

It is important however to mention that moderation in any physical discipline is vital in the longevity of the student. Many conservatories or university dance programs have students scheduled for as many as 4 classes a day. Although I myself was trained this intensely, I feel it is up to the teacher to take this into consideration when structuring a class. It is therefore imperative that the teacher be fully aware of whom they are teaching and have a sweeping knowledge of the technique and its possibilities, so as to provide a clear and thoughtful Horton experience.

---

[60] According to Alexander, bodies can be divided into four movement types, Swing, Release, Suspension and Shape.
[61] Dance Technique of Lester Horton, Page 108-113

Horton for the Practicing Professional: The benefits of the technique for company class.

In my experience as a professional dancer[62], I have found that the most integral part of the rehearsal day was my company warm up. As company teacher for many companies including Matthew Bournes', " New Adventures in Motion Pictures[63]' and Phoenix Dance Theater, I have used the technique as a training and performance enhancing tool, not only noticing the benefits during long rehearsal periods, but in the performances themselves.

I have discovered that although the design of a class for students has its training benefits, for professionals it has been beneficial to incorporate influences from other techniques as well, to give a well rounded warm up and training experience. I have found it necessary to intersperse the "Basic 7" with elements of the Graham contractions, and the Limon release theories, It has proven to balance the intensity of the linear and muscular emphasis of the Horton technique with simple swing and weight transference. It is however necessary to distinguish between these different techniques and styles to maintain the clarity and integrity of their principals. In the company class setting, over working a particular muscle group should be avoided, therefore if I was to give the full Flat back series and then Release Swings, I would perhaps not to give Fortification Number 1[64] (The Achilles Tendon Stretch) or Fortification Number 9 [65](The Split Stretch), as these combined would over exert the Hamstrings. Instead, it may be beneficial to start work on the Hinge Studies, or the preparation for the Stag position on the floor, perhaps even Fortification Number 2[66], which focuses more on the stretch of the thigh and shin muscles. Working on anatomical balance in a professional setting is vital in preparing the dancer for their rehearsal day.

---

[62] My career began with the Alvin Ailey Repertory Ensemble, Elisa Monte Dance, Ballet Hispanico, Complexions Contemporary Ballet, the Jose Limon Dance Company and Phoenix Dance Theater

[63] Adventures in Motion Pictures, a dance company, was founded in 1987 by British Dancer and Choreographer Matthew Bourne after he graduated from the Laban Centre in south London.

[64] Refer to page 54-56 of The *Dance Technique of Lester Horton.*

[65] Refer to page 67-68 of *The Dance Technique of Lester Horton*

[66] Refer to page 56-58 of *The Dance Technique of Lester Horton*

In a company setting, the dancers are of very different backgrounds and training, very few have even heard of the Horton technique, so in my experience it seems better not to include Fortifications or Studies unless the teacher can invest a longer period of time with the particular group of dancers or until the understanding of the shapes and their extremes have been realized. I think it is important that the teacher have a basic knowledge of the company's goals and expected repertory for the season therefore classes can cover as much of the principals of the technique as possible. Bear in mind the short amount of time a dancer has to warm up, usually an hour and a half, sometimes two and that simplicity in a Horton class structure can be as beneficial if not more so than a complicated and cluttered one.

One of the benefits of Horton as a training tool, is the all round strength it provides the body. Often muscles are used and engaged that the dancer has never worked. I find with professionals that fatigue plays a large part in injury and the implementation of Horton in a class brings internal focus to the body, which may create a greater awareness of weaknesses. The technique is an evolving technique and is therefore useful for teachers to harness as a creative tool to experiment and develop with professionals, so long as it is clear what the experiment is for.

It becomes important again to reiterate that the Horton technique is a lyrical technique[67], and although it has clear defined shapes, the professional should understand that it has to keep a sense of freedom that will also assist the dancer in utilizing a broader sense of movement, timing and artistry. Lester Horton, according to Carmen de Lavallade[68], preferred dancers who had to work harder because he felt the work and passion came from the emotional conquest. I do agree with him and, I find dancers with certain limitations, or short-comings often bring an edge to their work, and it appears as if they are devouring the movement for fear it may devour them. Encouragement during the class is vital for it creates a sense of safety within the space. Often teachers seem less concerned with the professional frame of mind relying on the fact that their experience has hardened them. In many cases, especially when confronted with a new movement vocabulary and physical rules, the professional can

---

[67] Lyrical movement, as in lyrical music refers to a fluid and continuous energy. Although rich in dynamics, it is not jarring or sudden in its approach.
[68] During a conversation held in New York City in July 2007.

feel overwhelmed and therefore visualization and imagery that he or she can easily connect to may be a better tool to achieve the technical outcome.

An image I use quite frequently when teaching, is the idea of, "eating up the space". It seems the animalistic quality of the Horton movement seems to rise out of the dancers, and they move bigger, cleaner, and more musically. This also allows them the freedom to let go of what they think the shape should look like, and truly experience it for themselves, with their knowledge, and their understanding.

I like to encourage dancers when attempting to learn a new technique, not to throw away what they already know, but to layer on what they would like to experience and achieve.

 The Horton technique was designed with the obvious idea that every body is made differently, even sometimes today we are faced with companies that produce or encourage a particular body type or aesthetic, The Horton technique does certainly produce a very particular body type. When taught incorrectly it can create an overly muscular dancer and often in the men it could mean over developed thighs, lateral torsos and muscular shoulders. In female dancers, there is the risk of an overly muscular back and smaller waists with more defined and larger thigh muscles. These are all to be considered when providing Horton as a company class for a ballet company, or one with a similar aesthetic. Here again a thoughtful class structure is important, and Ballet dancers have a keener sense of their own physical capabilities and goals and therefore, when taught correctly, the technique can provide more refined and powerful possibilities for their dancing. It is also important to mention that when working with predominantly ballet trained dancers, the over use of hyperextension which they may have under control in their ballet classes, may be exaggerated while in the Horton class. Bring awareness to the use of the inner thigh and pelvic floor lengthening upwards, and the slight shift of the weight forward over the toes. This should help to re align the dancers personal body knowledge with the Horton aesthetic.

After my experience as company teacher for the UK based, Phoenix

Dance Theater in 2007, as it was there first experience with the technique I tried to ease them into the shapes and principals. Being a dancer with the company as well gave me a stronger sense of the demands of the repertory which, at that stage, consisted of works by Artistic Director, Javier De Frutos[69], works by Jose Limon and Jane Dudley[70], who's solo, "Harmonica Breakdown" has a very strong Graham foundation. I had the dancers usually twice a week for an hour and a half over the course of 5 months. The dancers ranged in age from 22-31 years old, with very diverse training and professional backgrounds[71]. I did not teach any Fortifications or Preludes in their entirety, but focused more on defining the shapes and aesthetics of the technique.

At the end of the 5 months I handed each a questionnaire to assess what were found to be beneficial as well as challenging aspects of Horton as a company class.

When asking them to discuss what they found the differences were between Horton and the techniques they had studied, the majority found the shapes very precise and the lines very clear to strive for. There were no differences between responses from male or female dancers, all found it beneficial for its co-ordination skills, the focus placed on working in parallel and turn out simultaneously was a challenge, but the linear quality helped to focus the energy out of the body.

The benefits listed mostly included strength in the lower back and Hamstring and clarity of energy flow from the floor through the arms and top of the head, particularly in the Flat Back. The most

---

[69] Javier De Frutos was born in Caracas, Venezuela in 1963 where he began his dance training. He went on to study at the London School of Contemporary Dance and in New York at the Merce Cunningham studio and with Barbara Mahler and Sara Rudner. In 1989, he joined Laura Dean Dancers and Musicians and in 1992, he was appointed Choreographer in Residence at Movement Research in New York City.

[70] Dudley was born in New York City, and studied dance with Hanya Holm, Louis Horst, and Martha Graham. Between 1937 and 1944 she was a leading dancer in the Martha Graham Company. In 1970 she moved to London to teach at London Contemporary Dance. She died at age 89.
[71] The company had ex-dancers from; Netherlands Dance Theater 2, New Zealand Ballet, Rambert Dance Company and Merce Cunningham Dance

challenging for the dancers was the "Lateral T" and "Back T" shapes as well as Lateral T turns, and the opposition of the Parallel leg versus the turned out leg in the "T" shape.

I found in the questionnaires that all the dancers listed Laterals as one of the more beneficial exercises, the woman stated that it helped their partnering skills by strengthening their core muscles and allowing them to control their upper bodies better. The men stated that the stabilization of the legs and pelvis helped to ground them better in partnering.

When asked whether they noticed any enhancements to there artistic or performance growth, they all agreed that more time was needed to become comfortable with the shapes.

As a concert dancer I use company class as a way to re evaluate and reconstruct my technique, so it does make sense that the performance aspect may not be so vital a goal for the practicing professional.

One of the most beneficial preparations it seems in a Horton based company class, is the Elementary Balance Study[72]. I taught this in sections, and then created variations on positions and transitions. The dancers responded well, and commented that it helped with the carriage of weight making it more controlled and confident, as well as refining the bodies' alignment most effectively.

These comments were similar when I taught a Horton based company classes for Matthew Bourne's, " Adventures in Motion Pictures", the company has mostly ballet based training, with large amounts of Jazz and Cunningham. I was surprised that both companies had almost the same comments and experiences with Horton.

As with students and younger dancers, the nurturing of professionals is as important, and can be maintained by setting clear goals for them in the Horton class. While the use of the Fortifications, preludes and Studies are invaluable and necessary for the training of students it seems after a period, the professional needs another creative aspect to the technique. It is wonderful for me to study and observe with

---

[72] Refer to page 78-79 of The Dance Technique of Lester Horton.

master teachers like Ana- Marie Forsythe and Milton Myers who have such an innate understanding of Horton's work that their combinations have the feeling that it would have come straight from Horton's imagination onto his dancers. I think in order to keep the technique alive, teachers should be encouraged to sometimes think outside the constraints of counts and directions and shapes, and remind the dancer of the endless possibilities and creative ideals of the Horton technique. It did after all develop from choreographic and performance ideas. I have found it helps the dancer to see the potential and where a particular shape can go. For example, when teaching Lateral T, I would also demonstrate a Lateral T Turn, a Lateral T Jump and a Lateral T Fall, these physical goals I have found help the dancer to understand the energy and placement value as well as the direction the shape can take.

Dance Class Etiquette

There are many important aspects to dance training and technique that can lay the groundwork for a successful and fulfilling dance career. An important aspect often over looked is that of basic classroom etiquette or behavior.

With working environments being so diverse, especially in the dance world, the basic respect and understanding among co-workers can often directly affect the work itself. I have found that through my own training and performing and now my position as director and teacher, it seems very necessary to lay down some basic guidelines for students when taking class or rehearsals.

 The encouragement of a dress code is certainly a practice which is quite varied amongst schools and learning institutions. I for example, had a strict dress code for dance classes at my performing arts school in South Africa[73]. Of course during my schooling it seemed like an unnecessary enforcement of conformity, but as I progressed through my training, it seemed apparent that the true education was that of self-respect. No matter what my socio-economic background or my sentiments about my body image were on any given day, I strived to have an impeccable uniform. Each grade had a distinctive color to differentiate our year of training, and I began to feel proud to wear my red colored tights which indicated I was getting ready to graduate.

The dress code became a way for me to feel proud of my art form, my discipline, and my body. As a teacher in schools and universities around the world, I always request a copy of the dress code guidelines, if any, and try to encourage the students to wear their dress code with pride, and remind them that they can carry these lessons into life outside of dance. I like to think that the self-discipline and respect we learn in a dance class can be applied to any other work situation.

---

[73] I attended the National School for the Arts based in Johannesburg as a dance major from 1992-1997.

Personal hygiene is also important to include. As artists we are exposed to many different cultures and people with diverse backgrounds. I do feel that the studio is a sanctuary, a common space where artists combine and share themselves with each other, and eventually audiences. It is important to guide students to also respect one another by acknowledging their fellow dancers space, and making them feel as comfortable as possible.

One of my early memories of learning about etiquette was during a rehearsal for Swan Lake with Ms. Nicola Middlemist[74] from PACT Ballet in South Africa. She was the Ballet Mistress for the company, and was sent to my school to restage act 2 of the ballet for the dance department. I was 14, and even though I had been around dance and dancers since I was 4 years old, no one had ever told me that there were certain things you did and did not do when you were in a dance studio.

The first was to wash your hands before you partnered anyone. Ensure your tights were cleaned the night before, and that you had a pleasant body odor, and that you always had a towel in your dance bag to wipe up any excess sweat. This seemed like common knowledge, but because no one every told me up until then, I simply didn't think about that. As a professional dancer, it has served me well to be mind full of those things- I think it has left a good impression on the directors and fellow dancers I have worked with by showing my maturity and respect for my craft and my co-workers.

I recently had an experience when doing a ballet class in NYC. I was about to start the pirouette exercise, and we were preparing at the back of the studio to travel forward. As I was about to go, I made a grand gesture in my preparation. Suddenly a fellow student stepped directly in front of me and began to prepare herself. I was unable to take my turn. I am sure it was not done out of malice, as I did not know her, but she was simply unaware. This is an important element I like to instill in all my students. Be mind full of your surroundings,

---

[74] Ms Middlemist trained at the Royal Ballet School in London during the1960's. She was part of the pioneer group chosen by Dame Ninette de Valois for her teacher's course, later known as 'The Craftsman's Course'. After joining PACT Ballet, Nicola rose through the ranks from Corps de Ballet to Senior Soloist. In 1973 she embarked on a new career as Repetiteur, before progressing to Senior Ballet Mistress, a position she held from 1992 until the closure of the State Theatre in 2000.

not only to benefit your own expressiveness and openness, but also for the respect and encouragement of your fellow dancers. Know where you are, and make visual contact with the person, or persons you are about to dance with. It is simply another way to engage with the movement. Sharing that combination and that space with the dancers is a gift, and another way for me to refine my artistry. My goals when I take class include; connecting with my body, the choreography, the music, the emotion, and my fellow students.

Although these all seem simple, I have found that for myself, they make my classroom experiences as a student and teacher healthier, and more productive.

Suggestions for a Horton Class:

As I have previously mentioned, the Horton technique is an evolving training tool. It has a vocabulary, but as in poetry, the words can be arranged to best suite the outcome or intention of the work. I have included one of my basic lesson plans as well as a contribution by Ana-Marie Forsythe as examples of a class structure. Again these are only suggestions and we are always encouraged to be creative in our choices. More explanations of the fortifications and preparatory exercises can be found in the Horton textbook, The Dance Technique of Lester Horton published by Dance Horizons/ Princeton Book Company. I have included page numbers for better reference.

Aspects to include in a Horton Class –

a) Starting and ending each exercise in parallel to create muscular balance

b) Incorporating the basic elements of the Horton lines beginning with flat backs, then primitive squats, laterals, leg swings, metatarsal presses, lunges and dimensional tonus (the yawn stretch – Advanced classes)

c) Being Aware that in exercises where extreme stretches, sustained extensions or deep hinges are executed, the large grouped muscles — like those of the Quadriceps and the Gluteal may shake. This will become less noticeable as the strength in the weaker and supportive muscles improves.

d) The use of a swing series or rhythmic exercise after a sustained movement study, gives the body and mind the opportunity to re-energize.

e) Reminding the student never to treat an exercise as though it is just for strengthening or limbering a body part. Using each exercise to explore its expressive qualities this brings awareness to the performance aspect of the exercise

f) Taking chances as the class progresses, but not diminishing the focus on precision work.

g) Encouraging exploration or improvisation to awaken individual dancers' movement sensibilities.

h) Reminding the dancers to imagine the potential for each movement, not just the movement itself, but what that shape or step could become.

The introductory Horton class- (Based on a hour and a half class with students with little or no Horton experience, but intermediate Ballet training. This plan can also be followed for a single workshop, including elements of the Preludes and Fortifications)

This Horton class structure is based on what I consider to be important Horton principals to cover with dance students and professionals who have had limited or no exposure to the technique. I have structured this based on the understanding that the teacher has a firm grasp on the elements and requirements of the technique, and has considered and studied the Preludes, Fortifications and Studies on a full time basis. For dancers with more experience with the technique, many variations on the structure can be included to best suit the level and technical demands the dancers will face during the course of their rehearsal and performance days.

The Center warm up:

1) The Roll Down – Given in 4's and 2's in both parallel 2nd and first position (I have also included turned out 1st and 2nd positions, depending on the standing Preludes or Fortifications I will give). It is important to ensure that there is equal weight distribution on both feet while rolling up and down. Ensure that the abdominal muscles are engaged throughout the exercise.

2) Bounces in all positions- light and ensuring they do not pop or lock there knees- Ensure that the knees are directly inline with the top of the foot and Ankle. This would usually followed by Primitive Squat (Page 37)

3) Basic Spinal Twists – Including stationary Egyptian twists, then evolving into Egyptian Walks. Arches and Curls of the spine can also be included to articulate and warm the muscles surrounding the Vertebra and lower Lumbar region.

4) Flat Back Series in 3 (Page 31-35) –For beginners I would usually only go as far as the series with relevé, then followed directly with the roll downs and flat back recovery. I would wait to include the *Eleven 3's* series after a few more classes. The same applies to the introduction of the flat back, back bend (Pelvic Press).

5) Laterals (Page 31-35)– in 4, 2 and 1 counts. I start with single arms, then repeat with double arms. I also give a series including a full Plié and a horizontal change, possibly even a release of the head to the ankle to further stretch the back of the legs.

6) Pliés and Grande Pliés – to loosen the hips and prepare the hamstrings and knees for Release Swings.

7) Release Swings – (Page 38-39) Plain and with Torso. Again I would spend a few more classes with them before introducing the full circle.

8) Foot exercises, (Page 185-186)including ankle flexion and extension and Degagé. (I like to include basic rhythm combinations as well as increasing tempo.)
See Foot Isolations and Strengtheners.

9) Deep Lunge series. (Page 150-151)

10) Lateral T preparation- Bounces in to high lateral, both sides, in 8's. I progress it into Lateral T position on both sides.

11) Fortification #1. Achilles Tendon Stretch (Page 54-56)

(Fortifications # 2-4 can be taught in sections over a series of lessons) This helps to also work the parallel vs. turnout opposition.

12) Either Prelude # 1 (Page 99-100) or Elements of Elementary Balance (Page 78-79)
13) Parallel Leg Swings – (Page 47) low, medium and high, alternating legs. Ending in a stag position to introduce shape.
14) Coccyx Balance – (Page 91-94) simple series in 3 counts. Variations with leg and arm extensions can be introduced depending on level of students. As an aid for weaker abdominals, it can be taught with the hands on the floor.

Across the Floor:

1) Bounces and walks Introduced as an addition to the technique by Joyce Tristler. The legs start in natural second with the arms in high parallel. Torso bounces forward twice - 1,2 -reaching arms through the legs, legs are in plié or straight depending on the amount of Hamstring work you have given. Legs step right then left, arms are still in high parallel. Repeat across the floor. This I have found is a good way to introduce movement through the space after a series of center work.
2) Leg swings with Leg fans (an option if previous leg swings were not given) (Page 49)
3) Side Hip Pull. I often include a basic turning sequence of parallel and turned out pirouettes, repeat to other side. (Page 187- simple series)
4) Lateral T into cross lunge and pelvic press. Again playing with the shapes and transitions that I have already introduced, but now the potential development of each can be experienced by the student.
5) Single foot Arch Springs and jumps in 1st and 2nd (Page 196-198)
6) Moving Stag Progression – A simple pushing into space of the arms to achieve the stag position, moves across the floor alternating legs.
7) Combination – I usually give a short combination incorporating as many of the shapes and transitions that have been covered in the class.

Syllabus[75] for a 4 week workshop in Horton Technique for Advanced
Ballet Dancers. Contributed by Ana Marie Forsythe

The Horton Warm up

    Roll down, plié, straighten the knees, roll up

    Flat back series with variations

    Parallel bounces and Primitive Squat Descents and Ascents

    Lateral Stretches

    Release Swings

    Parallel Leg Swings

    Deep Lunges

Each of these elements of the Horton warm-up should be introduced
using the basic movements first and adding the variations as the
dancers feel comfortable enough to go to more advanced material.

WEEK ONE

The basic Horton Warm up

Center floor work should also include the following:

    Hip and rib isolations

    Torso Language

    Fortification # 1

---

[75] All of the material are taken from the Dance Technique of Lester Horton published
by the Princeton Book Company.

Elementary Balance

Lateral T position using the preparation for Lateral Side Twist Fall   phrases 1, 2 and phrase 3 through count 9, holding count 10 in relevé

Coccyx Balance

Progressions

Leg swings

Side hip pull

Cross lunge

Combinations of movements using the progressions above

Single foot arch springs

WEEK TWO

Basic Horton warm up including some variations

Center floor work

Fortification # 14

Prelude # 3

Pivotal descent and ascent

Coccyx Balance with variation

Progressions

Leg swings with variations

Lateral T traveling

Sliding Descent

Combinations including progressions and movements previously covered.

Single foot arch springs

WEEK THREE

Horton warm up with variations

<u>Center floor work</u>

    Fortification # 3 and # 4

    Figure 8 hip isolations

    Coccyx Balance with variations

    Preparation for Side fall and Side fall from standing.

<u>Progressions</u>

    Leg swings with variations

    Twist hip turn

    Combinations combining progressions that were previously covered

    Single foot arch springs

    Skips

WEEK FOUR – review and clarifications

Basic Horton warm up with variations

<u>Center floor work</u>

    Hip isolations

    Fortifications # 1, 3, 4, 14

    Coccyx Balance

<u>Progressions</u>

Leg Swings with variations

Stag turns

Combinations of progressions previously covered

Single foot arch springs

Skips or leaps

Teaching is a building process, building vocabulary by repetition and experience. This syllabus is a suggestion and only a guide. Each instructor must use their experience and judgment about how quickly to move through the Horton material and measuring how quickly their students achieve command of the vocabulary. Some movements will take longer to achieve then others, but this guide should be accessible to most dancers with intermediate to advanced ballet training.

As I have mentioned previously, Horton developed shapes, ideas and movements over a period of time. He encouraged his students and company members to investigate the possibilities of each movement and their progressions. It is better to start with a simple idea and to clarify and encourage the technique to grow in a dancer's body. A structured Horton class should retain the principals of the technique but encourage the freedom of expression and exploration. There are many variations and possibilities one can include in a class. I would recommend a year of Horton training 2-3 times a week is ideal for a beginner before the dancer can begin to safely, and effectively master the principals and shapes required for the more advanced studies. This often does depend on the individual dancer, and the level of training the teacher is providing.

'The technique began to develop. The method was, I think, typical of the day. Lester would start a movement going and then build on it. He would start a movement pattern and then react to what he saw us do. The minute the dancers would feed him, he would bounce back on an elaboration of the theme. He would constantly challenge this level of movement- go further, go deeper.'[76]

Bella Lewitzky

---

[76] *A Vision of Total Theater*, By Bella Lewitzky. Dance Perspectives 31 Autumn 1967. P 47

CHAPTER 4
THE PERFORMANCE TECHNIQUE OF
LESTER HORTON

Defining the Energy Source.

In scientific terms, an energy source refers to matter or a system from which one or more forms of energy can be obtained[33]. Many people fail to see dance as a science, a vehicle for the direction of energy and matter through space and time. The term, Physical science is an encompassing term for the branches of natural science and science that study non-living systems, in contrast to the biological sciences. However, the term "physical" creates an unintended, somewhat arbitrary distinction, since many branches of physical science also study biological phenomena. It is strange to me that the term "non-living" is associated with the term physical, as it is clear in the minds and bodies of a dancer that being physical clearly makes us alive.

Dance is a biological phenomenon. It involves all the systems, actively and in co-ordination to create an energy source which affects all it comes in to contact with, therefore it makes sense to define it's energy or life-giving source.

The basic distinctions in the direction of energy focus within dance technique give a deeper sense and understanding of the driving force behind a movement. The basic elements associated with dance include; The Body, it's Actions, Dynamics, Relationships and Space. Dance composition should include climax and resolution, contrast, repetition, sequencing and development, transition, unity, and variety.

The Alexander Technique[34] refers to body types with the basic principals of momentum; such as shape, release, suspension and swing. Many of us posses one or more of these in the natural way we move our bodies. Most of the early dance techniques were similar in

[33] Definition according to the online, Wikipedia reference tool.
[34] The technique takes it's name from F Matthias Alexander who developed his technique of body reeducation and co-ordination through physical and psychological principals between 1890-1900. The technique focuses on the self-perception of movement and is promoted for the alleviation of back pain, rehabilitation after accidents, improving breathing, playing musical instruments and singing.

how they shaped the human body, but to distinguish themselves from one another, the energy initiation and sometimes its direction had to change. Some pioneers of modern dance had extensive exposure to each other, some had little or non. Even with these factors, the natural or biological movement explorations found in the body where almost identical within these modern techniques. It is therefore safe to assume that physical explorers like Martha Graham, Jose Limón, Lester Horton and Merce Cunningham all experienced the same potential in the body, but sought to differentiate their findings so as too broaden the creative possibilities of their art form and therefore distinguish themselves from each other.

An example is the Abdominal Contraction. More strongly associated with the Graham technique, and when executed in the Graham style, is an active drawing in and up of the abdominal wall, causing the spine to lengthen and the torso to round forward. In the Cunningham technique, it is simple known as a curve, which is a passive rounding of the upper torso in either direction. Limón calls it a forward bend, again the emphasis is on the weight of the head creating the shape, therefore it becomes a passive movement, and the energy is caught at the bottom of the shape and is replenished on the way back to the neutral spine. In a Horton class, it is simply known as an "abdominal lift", again it is safe to say that each has the same physical outcome, but a very different way of expressing or executing the energetic momentum.

Considering Horton's work was based in California on the west coast of the United States, it would have been very easy for Horton to stay unaffected or un-influenced by the dance pioneers on the east coast of the US. However his observations and interests in movement and the organic possibilities of the human body, would not have allowed him to ignore the experimentation that was going on.

When discussing the differences and similarities between the modern techniques, it is easy to see the variations in their focus as early on in the class as the warm-up. In the Graham technique for example, the strength and dramatic quality of the movement takes is energy from the ground. Therefore it makes sense for almost all Graham classes to start seated on the floor, drawing from the earth up through the body, with its focus on the back and hips (Graham technique was however originally taught at the Ballet bar, when the company was all women).

Cunningham technique usually starts standing with emphasis on the arms and back as well as torso opposition, here it can be noted that although Cunningham, a brief student of Horton's in California, was one of Martha Graham's more distinguished and accomplished male dancers, his technique has often been described as the, "anti-Graham", because of the use of linear movement and lack of contraction initiations. Jose Limón's principals of sequential movement draw from the idea of weight and its distribution through the body into the floor. Therefore, in the Limón warm up, the dancer can either start standing or in some cases lying with their backs on the floor and focusing on the movement of the bones as opposed to the muscles.

In Contrast, the Horton technique is primarily a linear technique, comprising of the idea of straight lines of energy and alignment of the bones. It is safe to say that the body is strongest when all the bones are in one straight line. In architectural terms, the same would be the case if a beam or column holding up the roof of a building had a break or bend, this would be classified a weakness in the structural integrity of the building.

The principal of a linear technique is that energy flows from the center of the body (considered to be the abdominal region in most techniques) through all extremities in a straight line, with the same intensity, at the same pace. The idea is not to confuse the body in its pursuit for the illusion of length, and therefore in the Horton technique, the parallel relationship between the arms is so important in creating the direction of the energy flow either upwards or outwards. In the legs, the image of extending or planting the legs into the earth when combined with the length of the arms in opposition, has shown to provide more stability in the standing leg. This thereby helps to support the axis of the pivoting joints, such as the hip and thigh joint, in the Lateral T shape. With all of this, it seems the science of dance should have a sense of balance, identical to what is found in nature. Without opposing energies or phenomenon, like gravity, a dancers worst and best friend, we would not be able to execute anything consistently. Essentially, without the understanding of where you are coming from in the movement, you will then not be clear as to your destination or eventual outcome. I always say to my students, "Balance comes from opposition". Again gravity makes it clear to us, " What goes up, must come down", and so in the opposition of movement, what goes down, has the potential to rise up again and be rejuvenated. I tell my students to give their bodies somewhere to move from, especially in static or still positions, energy is infinite in its outcome, and even when still, the potential energy is active in the body.

In Horton, the shape is the starting position, and the clarity in the direction of energy in that shape provides the constant striving for length in all directions. This gives the body its starting point, as well as its potential energy and a definitive outcome.

An image I have often referred to when trying to get my point across involves the Butterfly Effect. Hypothetically, according to this scientific theory, when a Butterfly flaps its wings in India for example, a tornado occurs off the coast of California. The idea is that the energy created by the smallest creature does not simply dissipate; it grows, and when combined with other natural forces, has the potential to culminate into something catastrophic.

If one considers that the head is the heaviest part of the body, any action it makes, has a definite reaction to the rest of the body, the relatively small amount of energy exerted by dropping the head forward with the chin to the chest, has the potential for a large disturbance of the balance of the body, particularly if on relevé, therefore the same butterfly theory can be applied to the body. Technique is about learning to control the body, and its energy direction, and not allowing the body to dictate or control the dancer, this varies in teachings and styles of dance such as Release Technique[35], where the body is the driving force behind the projection of energy through the space.   If not channeled thoughtfully, the energy output creates an inconsistent outcome. The idea of a linear spine in the Horton technique allows for this consistent emoting of energy outwards in all directions even in twists or Lateral positions. This linear design allows for multi-directional

---

[35] Release technique is a dance technique that emphasizes the body's natural alignments and movements. It is based on lack of tension, utilizing breath and momentum to facilitate movement. This is in contrast to other dance techniques that encourage distortion of the body's natural alignments or movements by force.

energy which never returns to the body, but is consistently re-
generated from its core. Therefore Horton has the potential to
become a three dimensional technique and this multi directional
approach allows for a stabile foundation in the body while
maintaining the freedom to explore

In contrast in the Limón technique, energy is generated then expelled,
caught then released, defining itself as an exploration in "fall and
recovery". The energy is created as the weight is dropped
downwards, this allows for a falling of the energy sequentially
through the body, as it reaches the bottom- and before it dissipates- it
is recovered and traced back through the same channels of the body
allowing the weight to be shifted through the space dynamically and
facilitating a reaction in the rest of the body. There is a definite
momentum and when executed correctly a sense of "free fall" which is
without a driven force, but instead rides on the initial energy action.

In the Graham technique, the emphasis is on circular energy flow.
After the energy is directed out of the body through the rounded
movement or contraction, it is returned to the body making the shape
stronger and therefore more dynamic. The abdominal contraction is a
primary focus in this technique. It allows for a flow of energy that is
powerful and dynamic at the start, and then through a consistent
flow, the depth of the movement is increased and is continuously
being fed and rejuvenated by this circular pattern of energy. The
oppositional forces are more internal than external, and an image
often used to help understand the concept, is that of two opposing
sides of a curve moving in different directions from there base, but
the ends are moving towards one another.

Figure 26. A Cunningham lifted Curve

The abdominals are active and pulling inwards towards the spine as well as Upward towards the throat.

Figure 27. A Limón forward curve.

This shape relies on the weight of the head, it is therefore passive, but has an internal energy. The shoulders remain over the hips.

Figure. 28 – Cunningham Upper Curve and Graham Pleading Contraction

In Figure 28. above, the two opposing sides of a curve in the standing Cunningham upper curve, and the Graham pleading contraction are paralleled. They both have an active circular energy.

As a reminder, in the Horton Technique, while there is no "contraction" as in the Graham Technique, there is the use of a rounded back. In Horton, a contraction of the abdominal wall is known as an *Abdominal Lift*, this makes it clear to the dancer as to what part of the body to focus on, and the direction of the line of energy.

Cunningham's focus is similar to Horton in it's Linear structuring of the body, however it's focus seems to be more on the opposition of torso to limbs. There is a focus on standing with a third leg, or the idea of a midline passing through the body giving it a consistent upward and downward energy focus, as the limbs and torso move in opposing directions; forward, sideways, backwards and with twists.

Figure 29. The Midline, with oppositional energy focus in a Horton natural second Position.

Figure 30. In a Cunningham Tilt, the midline remains.

It appears that in differentiating amongst the modern techniques, we find similarities in their objectives. All are trying to create the illusion of length by extending the energy out of the body and, through opposition, provide a balance and a dynamic performing quality which will enhance the students understanding of the movement. The clarity of Horton's technique in achieving this is remarkable and could be why Ballet trained dancers adapt so easily to the Horton technique. Ballet also has a sense of outward projective energies to achieve length and balance. Horton, Cunningham and Ballet are all shape orientated techniques, whereas Limón, Graham and Release are energy initiated.

I feel it is important to teach about energy and its direction in dance because it is such an integral part of performance and assists in the correct development of the body. I have found that in Horton, because there is a constant lengthening of the muscles, it also aids in preventing some of the basic injuries prone to the difficult physical aspects of the technique. This constant attainment of muscular length through the focusing of energy direction, assists the body in not becoming heavy or fatigued during strenuous performance activities.

The Theory of Push and Pull Energies

Another aspect to energy variation is something I like to call the "Push and Pull Theory". All pedestrian movement has an action or initiation and a reaction or direction. It seems important then to apply the same organic logic to the differentiation in the focus of dance movement. I also work with Ascending, Descending or lateral energies, specifically when analyzing turns in Horton.

Dancers have a more specific outcome to their movement choices, at least in the technical training, and therefore an understanding in the differentiation between active and passive energies, or "push and pull" energies, will aid the dancer in their comprehension of dynamic energy flow. This is particularly apparent in the Horton aesthetic.

Push energy includes all active initiations in the body, with an active and consistent continuation as one would experience while pushing something heavy. The whole body is involved and the weight is placed onto the object. In dance, I like to think of space as our most important prop. It can be moved in all directions, and filled or emptied of intention, energy, and emotion. In order to move through space, the back and the torso play an important part as they control and initiate the energy and propulsion of the body in all directions. Push movement, can also often be accented or be given a sharper dynamic to the body as the initial surge of energy places the body on alert. Michio Ito's influence in Horton's early training encouraged him to develop the attention and refined use of the torso and arms, this can still be seen today in the careful and thoughtful placement of the arms in relationship to the back, and the initiation and balance of the movement. The Push quality gives the arms weight, and the torso and back a larger shape. In the legs, the opposition of pushing down through the feet to transfer the weight gives the movement a grounded and more stable base.

Pull energy has an active initiation, but a passive continuation i.e. the initial force is great, but the outcome relies on weight and is determined by the force of the original movement. Pull energy also relies on the oppositional forces, almost like those found in a rubber band. When the energy is pulled in one direction, an equal and sustained force is lengthened away from it, in the opposite direction.

All movement can fall into both of these categories, depending on how they are approached and this would fall into lateral energy focus. A movement like the Side Hip Pull, can be achieved with the emphasis both on push and pull ideals, as well as the Descending energy approach however, with the Pull Theory applied, it has a more suspended feeling, and with the Push Theory, the dynamic is more weighted, and the hip and arms have a sharper initiation.

With regard to Ascending or Descending energies, a prime use is in differentiating the Horton Turns. For example, a descending turn like a pirouette has the emphasis on the energy going up and being sustained, there is still oppositional energy pressing down into the floor through the feet, and down the back through the arms but, the focus is to sustain the multiple turns up. Descending turns, like, *Figure Four turn*, relies on the spiraling of the energy downwards through the standing leg, the turn therefore finishes in a descended position. I encourage my students to analyze whether turns are Ascending, descending or lateral, I have found this gives them a better understanding of how to initiate, where to sustain and how to end.

Musicality.

Horton's creativity, as previously discussed, was ignited by his lifelong interest in American-Indian[36] cultures. Their history, dress, food and above all music became the driving force behind some of his most passionate and ingenious works. The virtuosity and dynamics of his technique, which is further enhanced by its lyrical qualities, allows for the dancer to investigate musical nuance and differentiation in the execution of the exercises.

During the course of studying the technique, I have had the opportunity to work with phenomenal musicians who, through the guidance of the master teachers, have developed a clear musicality, which is integral in the teaching of the technique to students. I have found it necessary but not imperative to have live accompaniment for class it makes it easier because Horton loved diminishing counts. There are many exercises which may start in a 12 for example, and then as it is repeated, the counts reduce to 8 counts and 4 and so on. This clarity of rhythm allows for an easier assimilation of the shapes and execution, as the first slow and perhaps more lyrical structure is built into a faster and more dynamic movement. This appears to improve the clarity of muscle actions and reactions.

There are many studies in the technique that make use of complicated rhythmical variations, these help the dancer to stay alert, and cultivate a more creative sense of musical expression. In beginner classes however, the musician is encouraged to play rhythms which are less complicated, so as to assist the student in becoming accustomed to moving within the musical structure and, help them to be comfortable and confident with their own music expression. In the intermediate and advanced classes, the full range of Horton's musical expectations are realized.

A prime example, is the Dimensional Tonus or Yawn Stretch which consists of three 8's, two 10's, four 7's, two 4's, two 9's, four 3's, two 9's and then 16 counts. These would be very difficult to achieve without a live percussionist, as the quality is long and sustained.

[36] Native Americans in the United States are the indigenous peoples from the regions of North America now encompassed by the continental United States, including parts of Alaska and the island state of Hawai'i.

Another example is Fortification # 2, the Plié Study[37] which is broken down into; nineteen 3's, four 2's, three 3's, four 2's, eight 3's, four 4.s, 12 counts, and four 4's. These are just two examples of the complexity and dynamic variations created within a Horton class.

I think it is important to encourage young dancers to expose themselves to as many different styles of music, not only to enhance there understanding of melody, rhythm and dynamics, but to also place emphasis on the necessity for musical sensitivity.

Horton often made use of his company dancers to create and play the music to accompany performances; this must have given them a better understanding of the nuances of the movement, and the importance of audible artistry. With this in mind, I feel percussion music best suites a Horton class. The rhythm, drive and traditional implications of drum music provide a clearer initiation in most of the Horton Studies. I have had classes accompanied by piano, and again, the lyrical quality of Horton is enhanced, and it seems more noticeable when a piano is driving the body. Traditional classical music does not provide the necessary rhythmical qualities for the performance and execution of the technique, therefore pianists who are capable in improvisation, and experimentation are always encouraged.

Of course, if you do manage to find a jewel of a musician who can provide both percussion and piano, then the movement, and the dancers seem to take on a life of their own. I have included my interview with Victor See Yeun[38], a leading figure in the development of music for the Horton class. Victor has been involved in dance since the seventies as stage manager and lighting director for The Hummingbird Dance Company N.Y.C.; Victor is an accomplished interpretive improvisationalist, playing musical styles from jazz to rock, rhythm and blues to classical, country and western to reggae, calypso to pop, soca to rap, West African to funk, folk to salsa, and gospel to world music.

I asked Victor to explain his relationship to the Horton technique as

---

[37] The Dance Technique of Lester Horton, page 56-58

[38] Victor is a songwriter, record producer, arranger, and poet, and has mixed and mastered many outstanding albums and CD recordings. He is president and co-founder of the organic percussion ensemble "Heritage O.P." Victor's duet CD releases with William Catanzaro "Evolution Suites" and there latest 2007 release "Percussion for the Dance Technique of Lester Horton" includes a 16 page instructional booklet writing by Ana Marie Forsythe.

well as the relationship between Horton and music. These where his responses:

1. Q: How long have you been playing for the Horton Technique?

    A: I have been playing music for the Lester Horton dance technique for the last 20 years and counting. I didn't know of Lester Horton before I came to Alvin Ailey as a substitute drummer, when the school was on Broadway at 44th Street in NYC. Before Alvin Ailey, all my drumming and percussion was done with music groups, orchestras, and drum and dance African ensembles.

2. Q: What elements do you find in the technique, if any, that enhance   your   playing?

    A: The following list shows how elements of the Horton technique have enhanced my technique: (1) learned to groove through the odd counts within each exercise. (2) Able to accent when necessary to add to the drama and excitement of the exercise. (3) Developed a unique style of playing by making it easier for the teacher, student or listener to be able to know where the one count is, and how to flow with the drum music as if I'm also dancing to that particular exercise myself. (4) I listen to the counts and the inflection of the instructor's voice, and I get a musical impression instantly, and this allows me to play a rhythm or combination of patterns that I believe fits like a glove, making the music and dance, one. I ask you; what would music be without dance, and what would dance be without music? 20 years ago when I played for classes, I would rely on the rhythms I learned before and tried to make them fit into the Horton technique. Many times they didn't work and weren't appropriate, so I had to develop a style that would fit and make sense to the dancer and to myself. Now 100% of what I play for the Horton exercises and combinations are all improvisational and original rhythms.

3. Q: How important is the relationship between music and movement in the Horton technique?

A: A relationship is built between a dancer and a musician because the Horton technique is so precise, the lines are so clear and the shapes and angles are geometrically correct. As Ana Marie Forsythe would say, " It's either right or wrong no ifs or buts about it". Because of the Horton technique, the teachers and dancers who diligently made me part of their world throughout the many years, I was encouraged to record some music to preserve the technique even more. This process took 10 years, during which I figured out what exactly I should be doing and how to do it. During these times of creativity I didn't consciously listen to other artist's music, because I wanted to keep the Horton music that I was creating as pure as possible. Each CD started out with a concept first, and then the music was written around the concept, to give the dancer a bigger variety of music and a library of percussive knowledge to choose from. It was purposely done this way to keep the listener always coming back for more. Just like in Horton Movement, the sustained and continuous movement keeps the dancer growing and learning in each shape- there is always room for more, this is why the dancer/musician relationship is so important- the exploration of movement is more exiting when done together.

4. Q: Do you feel it is important for a Horton teacher to have a basic knowledge of music?   Do you think the music in a Horton class can be a good training tool for a young teacher?

A: (a) For a teacher to have a basic knowledge of music certainly helps, but as long as the teacher knows how to count from one to eight, they can make a living. Some teachers do not have the luxury to have a live accompanist in their classes, that's why it's important that the teacher understands how to make better choices in picking their music for the class, and how to take their students on a journey throughout the class with their teaching technique and with great music. It's important as a teacher to be able to give as much as he or she can, regardless of their musical background. Once the technique is taught correctly, the dancer will get it because as I was told, Lester Horton did some of his exercises in silence. But he loved music so much that he would use many different styles of music for his performances, crossing color boundaries and being innovative at the same time.   Most of the Horton works are in two's, three's, four's, six's and occasionally five's and seven's, sometimes different meters are all mixed up, to keep the brain active. This adds to the excitement and shows the dancer how complex a person Horton was and yet how simple. The CDs Percussion for the Dance Technique of Lester Horton Volume One and Volume Two certainly help the teacher and dancer to recognize the different meters. The introductions, double time, half time, change of tempos, the slow and fast tempos, and all the small nuances that are within the music keep it interesting and fun.

(b) I certainly think that the music for the Horton classes can be a learning tool for the younger and older teacher and dancer alike. When I first decided to record a CD of percussion music for the Horton technique, I started to put rhythmic patterns together for each particular exercise that flowed through my mind to give each exercise its own identity. That way, when a dancer hears a certain rhythmic pattern that I play, he or she knows exactly what exercise is being performed at the time. This technique has brought me closer to meditate on Lester Horton's thinking process, on what he might of envisioned and what musical sounds he could have been hearing at the time he was creating his masterpieces. I have learned about a technique that I normally would not have been exposed to, and it has made me a better musician and teacher. Therefore, I believe that the longer a dancer, student or teacher stays with the technique the more they will improve at it, because it gets imbedded in their spirit and touches their inner emotions. The automatic response is to smile, feel complete, inspired and fulfilled. This technique is safe anatomically and yet challenging for the dancer, and to have survived over 50 years since Horton's passing, the torch has been lit and is being passed on from generation to generation.

5.   Q. How would you explain the concept of dynamics to a student   of   dance?

A: Explaining the concept of dynamics to a dance student would have to be: (1) Listening to the music for the softness and loudness; (2) Live the music by using breath, action, stopping and starting, building a range from nothingness to a climax; (3) Every movement means something, so what's your story?, make it come alive to let the onlooker experience a part of you, in other words, be yourself; (4) Sometimes you have to come out of the box for your own self-growth and more times than not, you are happier that you did; (5) An artist has to take risks and step up to the plate to appreciate the challenges and adversity that come their way, and because of life lessons, the dynamics of a dancer becomes a universal embodiment encompassing every tear and joy; (6) Start simple yet know that the road to the meridian is a constant daily progress, one step at a time; (7) From tension to exaltation, from soft to hard, from quick to slow, what we experience in our daily lives, brings emotion to the classroom or stage and makes a believer out of me again and again.

Q: How much space for musical improvisation or creativity is there while playing for a Horton class?

A: For me, musical improvisation or creativity while playing for a Horton class is in everything I do. I know the technique very well, enough so that I can play with it by changing the rhythmic patterns within the one exercise or, by playing double time then going to half time and then double time again, just within a few measures if I so choose. I still hold on to the very musical quality as I push the envelope a bit to get the dancer to react to what I'm doing and to inspire them to be more of themselves by letting go. I can even correct the dancer verbally, whether he or she is doing the exercise correctly or not. I also challenge myself to play whatever the instructor wishes and at the pace he or she wants to move the class, I take my cue from the teacher and nine out of ten times, they allow me to play what I feel is right for the class. I spend a lot of time observing the behavior of the instructor, whether if it's the first class or the thousandth class to get a sense of what side of the bed they woke up on that day and how they want the class to progress, whether they had their coffee, they are in a good mood, they had breakfast, they had a good night's sleep. All this plays an important part in how the class will be, and when everything clicks and is in sync it gives the dancer a secure sense of accomplishment even after just one class or two. I love what I do, I live what I do, and I am what I do.

6. Q: Do you think rhythm and musicality can be taught?

A: Rhythm and musicality can definitely be taught. Take me for instance; I studied the American drum set from age 10. At age 18 I studied percussion and music for 4 years. How to play by myself, with someone else, with a percussion ensemble, with a music group, with an orchestra, with a vocal choir, with a brass ensemble, how to communicate with others even if no one speaks the same language, how to repair your own instrument when it's broken, how to make an instrument, how to listen to sound and identify it, and how to categorize it. Every country has a rhythm, and being born from that country you grow up hearing and living that rhythm, it becomes a part of your DNA musical makeup. The music we all grew up listening to and dancing to is different in many ways from country to country or even region to region. But we all have it deep inside us, that special spark, whether we wish to develop it or not is our prerogative. When we have that unconditional desire to pursue that dream of rhythm and music, only a few take that challenge or get that calling from that spiritual place within us, where no one can stop us, because it becomes bigger than life itself. When two or more musicians are working together each one has to be in sync with the other to be a part of a union that harmonizes sweet melodies and rhythms that are pleasing to the ear and heart. We walk in rhythm, we talk in rhythm, we move every part of our being in rhythm, we are rhythm, some are unaware of it but we are. Listen to our sweet musical heart beat, the drum beat of life, doop, deep, doop, deep, doop, deep, and not tick tock, tick tock, tick tock. Rhythm and music are everywhere in the universe, and if we are a part of the universe, then the universe is a part of us.

a. Q: As a music teacher, what 3 elements would you teach a student to best help them assimilate and interpret musicality?

A: As a music teacher, the elements that I would teach a student to best assimilate and interpret music are: (1) Listen to my CDs very carefully and take the time to understand each song with its sometimes simple and other times complex rhythms (when called for), because my CDs were designed to stimulate the dancer's spirit and conquer their inhibitions. (2) Healing music is another element that I would introduce to the student, because music in its true sense has been scientifically proven to heal the body and the mind. Music heals aches, tears, pain, suffering, and depression.   Just listening to beautiful music also brings joy, happiness, euphoria, peace and love. (3) Training the dancer/ student to pick out points of interest in the music and explore the possibilities, by physically reacting to the bass drum for instance or the triangle, or piano. I teach the student how to identify each instrument heard on the particular song and to sing back the melody or rhythm to me. I go from one instrument to the next until all of the instruments are identified and the dancer/student knows how all the different melodies and rhythms intertwine. In that way the student develops a better understanding of the structure of music and rhythm.

7.   Q: What can a teacher do to help YOU during a class?

A: What a teacher can do to help me when I'm playing for a class: (1) Give me a clear count off in the meter that the exercise is in; (2) If the teacher has a particular rhythm in mind, sing it to me, I'll play what he or she desires, I'm not a mind reader (yet); (3) Don't start counting in one tempo then slow down just before the down beat, because it confuses the musician who is getting ready to play. Sometimes the teacher gets excited and suddenly decides that the exercise calls for a slower/faster tempo, that's fine, just let the accompanist know by verbal counts, hand signals or body language. So just keep a steady count in what tempo you really want for the exercise; (4) If the teacher and musician are new to each other they should, whenever possible, communicate before class. They should talk about what the teacher is looking for from the musician and what the musician is looking for from the teacher in order to have a successful class; (5) If the teacher for some reason dislikes the musician and makes snide remarks about the musician in front of the students, the outcome can be disastrous; (6) A musician should never show any dislike of the teacher in front of any student, because it's unprofessional and shows a lack of discipline and respect; (7) A teacher can direct a musician by giving him or her a command directly or, indirectly by telling the student when the change in tempo or meter is coming up, and the musician will make the necessary adjustments to accommodate. (8) If a teacher likes what a musician is playing, he or she should let the musician know, because that comment reinforces that the musician is on the right track with the teacher and they are both going down the same path together; (9) Now if a teacher doesn't like what the musician is playing, the teacher should politely tell the musician to try another approach or give the musician a suggestion without belittling the musician (10) Each teacher and musician are in the same place for a reason, to have a great class together for the students, so it should be painless and fun for all.

10. Q: As a class accompanist what, if anything, has changed for you from when you first played for a Horton Class till now?

A: As a class accompanist, everything has changed for me from the time I first played for a Horton class until now, because I've evolved by not just getting older but by getting better. Practice makes perfect as the saying goes, but I do practice on my own, perfecting my drumming technique with no end in sight. I think of the class helping me in my musical preparation as if I'm performing in front of a live audience, so I fine-tune my craft right in front of the students and they don't even know it. I seldom make mistakes and when I do, because I stop concentrating for a moment, I know how to cover it up without anyone realizing that a mistake was made. I don't give it away by making any facial expression or indication that something went wrong. My playing has changed over the years, because I hear the music differently now, I have changed for the better, I hope. The past has encapsulated what I have accomplished, but I'm not the same person I was 20 or even 10 years ago. I see new possibilities and new accomplishments to achieve, you see, the journey is just beginning. I do not sit back and pat myself on the back, because there is a lot of work still to be done. And if I only have 60 more years to live, I have to start now, because time is priceless and too precious to waste. While working with groups in the past, I played rhythms I had learned, now I play all original rhythms for the classes, and in my opinion, it works.

11. Q: As a musician, what in your opinion are the benefits of the rhythmical and dynamic qualities of the technique for a dancer?

A: From my viewpoint as a musician, the benefits of the rhythmical and dynamic qualities of the Horton technique for the dancer are: (1) It increases the dancers' strength and teaches them how to manipulate body shapes to create new possibilities so that the technique can grow and blossom into something extraordinary. (2) It keeps the heart pumping strong, and that's a health benefit. (3) It creates the desire to see the technique performed well and when it is executed expertly, one never tires of watching Horton dancers perform. (3) It is easy to learn the beginning stage of Horton because of its simplistic structure. As the stages progress, the difficulty increases while still fortifying the body. (4) The entire body and mind work in unison when the dancer uses the Horton technique. Perfecting the technique comes with time.

12 Q: What about Horton inspires you?

A: Horton inspires me in many ways because of his legacy: (1) Horton loved percussion. I live it myself; (2) He and his dancers would make their own performance clothes. I sew as well; (3) The technique was developed on a stage without mirrors, in that way you had to feel what you were doing and be one with it. I feel the audience when I perform; (4) His Company members were very diverse, having many nationalities with different cultures. I'm also from a multi-cultural heritage; (5) Horton was all alone on the West coast where he developed his technique. It always inspired me because he didn't follow the crowd; there was no crowd to follow. Horton danced to his own tune, his own drum, his own calling and did it well.

William Catanzaro, and Argentinean born musician, and a Horton class accompanist at the Alvin Ailey School in New York as well as STEPS on Broadway believes, "Lester Horton understood music; he did not need external help like Martha Graham who relied on assistance from musician and composer Louie Horst for the development of her technique and choreography". It is for this reason that the Horton Technique gives a dancer; solid, rhythmical roots, but according to William, can also be a trap. " You have to be able to understand all aspects of music because, like life, there are many aspects to it". It is possible in Horton to be dependent on "the beat", it is much easier to experiment with musicality if you are clear with what the original beat is". It seems necessary at times then to encourage the use of a pianist; this may provide the dancer with variety in movement and dynamic experimentation.

There is no doubt that music played an important role in the development of Horton's choreography and technique. His keen interest and exploration of traditional rhythms and their structures through out his life, and the dedication he sought from his dancers in their understanding of musicality, created a physical vocabulary rich in dynamics, power and presence. Today's teachers and musicians who are educating another generation in the importance of musical sensitivity and possibility are carrying Horton's legacy forward.

Imagery and Mental Development

Dance imagery has been an important and somewhat overlooked aspect of training for many students and professionals. It becomes clearer as we progress through our lives, how important it is for us to set both mental and physical goals for ourselves to facilitate better outcomes for our lives. I think being such a physical art form; we sometimes overlook our mental and physiological development as an integral step in our development as artistic beings.

What is so apparent in the Horton technique, is that it is was an open technique, and was designed to be performed, this already establishes the foundations for professional dancers by placing the student automatically in the performance state of mind. When combined with the technical knowledge, it creates focus both internally and externally. Joyce Trisler when describing her first experience with Horton in 1950 said," The dancers seemed dressed for a performance, they were lit for a performance, and-though this was only a class-they went through it as if an audience were watching. Everyone was being trained to perform. It was a kind of controlled freedom, if there is such a thing. They didn't seem confined to any one level, but would swoop down on the floor, and miraculously end up soaring through the air."[39]

Dance has always been very goal orientated. We as dancers strive to perfect and refine our shapes and executions and as teachers we hope to attain the same for our students. What has been so motivating about my study of Horton, has been that it has allowed me to take note of my own progression and achievements. The rhythms and movements are exiting and dynamic, which energizes and moves me closer to my physical goals. It seems apparent, that because of the different physical initiations and co-ordinations, the body is encouraged to develop different neurological patterns and an increase in muscle memory. The importance of muscle memory for a dancer is priceless. We rely so much on our minds to assimilate steps, shapes and complicated choreographic patterns, that the sooner we can pass those on to our muscles, the quicker we can focus on something else, like performing.

Horton shape and movement is so clear that it seems to seep into the body quickly; again this leaves more room for the dancer to advance and I encourage dancers to move bigger the first time they learn or execute a shape. This physical commitment gives the body a chance to clarify the movement paths, as well as providing the mind with the opportunity to refine and create a memory pattern or movement association.

I often use the image of breathing; it is the prime example of muscle memory. When we are born, the first movement in our body is the contraction and release of the Inter-costal Muscles between the ribs; this is our first breath, and from then on, our most important

---

[39] The Magic and Commitment by Joyce Trisler. Dance Perspectives 31 (1967). Page 54

involuntary muscle action. The basic foundations are so apparent in the technique that, once clarified, it allows the muscles to retain the information, and gives the mind the opportunity to focus on something else. This is muscle memory!

Image driven choreography is a lot easier to pick up and I have found that in Horton, imagining and focusing on the direction of the energy enhances the bodies understanding thereof. Carmen De Lavalade has often said that Horton encouraged dance, "to become your work, there was no competition". I have heard her say ," Knock out your walls, give your body permission to leave the room[40]". I found myself dancing bigger, and the image of my body seemed broader in my head. I found that I ended up driving myself to attain and set higher physical and mental goals for myself in all my dance classes, not just Horton. This helped me to achieve more because I was asking my body to work deeper and clearer.

Process is as important, if not more so, than the final achievement. What makes the technique so inspirational is its accessibility for beginners as well. Ballet dancers, who have never experienced modern or contemporary dance, can connect more clearly to Horton because of its linear qualities. I like to encourage growth through process and I tell my students that it is more interesting to investigate how far you can take your body in a movement, and how intelligently you can maneuver inside a shape, then sometimes the actual shape itself. This I think is what separates a dancer from an artist. The Alexander Technique, often used to re-train or bring awareness to unnecessary or unconscious patterns in the body, refers to goal-orientated bodies as "End Gainers"[41]. I think in Horton, it is especially important to encourage the importance of process. Even though the studies are laid out to us with the counts and phrasing so clearly, it must be remembered that the design and initial inspiration behind them was investigation. How far can a movement be taken, this is more often a mental choice, then a physical one. Dance teaches tenacity, discipline and confidence, these should be instilled within our movement choices as well.

---

[40] In an interview with Ms. De Lavallade in New York City, July 2006
[41] End gaining is the tendency we have to keep our mind and actions focused on an end result whilst losing sight of, and frequently at the expense of, the means-whereby the result is achieved.

Bella Lewitzky has been quoted in a Horton class as saying, " carve out your space"[42], I think this is a fundamental principal of the Horton technique, the idea of physical and mental domination of space and weight. This gives a greater sense of performance and it changes us from a two dimensional shape to a multidimensional physical manifestation of energy.

I find that in striving for focus in dance, there is always the risk of negating or becoming detached from our other senses. I like to remind dancers to be aware of what they see, hear, smell and taste during the course of a dance class. I have even used unlikely images like tasting a movement as if it were a juicy strawberry, or a ripe melon, rather than a piece of dry stale bread. This amusing image often seems to add a more passionate or deeper execution of the movement and even the use of word association, and a simple concept of a summer fruit can add another layer. Don't be afraid to think unconventionally when it comes to movement imagery. One has to acknowledge that the body retains and is influenced by our early senses and what we experience externally. How often have we smelt something, or heard a tune that takes us back to an early memory. Why not let these human characteristics and feelings influence the way we move, it is after all what audiences really connect with, not the actual steps themselves, but how they feel after seeing them interpreted. These senses bring with them a sensitivity to the movement and the dancers surroundings and, have also proved to enhance mental imagery and physical nuance by bringing their consciousness into the room as well as into their bodies. I like to think of the technique providing the necessary tools to give the body permission to move. This, combined with the idea of continuous linear energy flow in all directions, makes the body and mind, "performance ready". Joyce Trisler recalls an early experience with Horton," One evening in rehearsal he (Horton) worked me into a rage to get me to throw myself into a lift. When it was over, he said, "Now remember what that feels like-not the rage, but the force it takes to get into the lift." The lift itself was rage when it was properly executed"[43]

---

[42] In an interview with Ms. De Lavallade in New York City, July 2006- She openly discussed her experiences with Ms Lewitzky as a teacher. Ms de Lavallade replaced Lewitzky in Horton's production of Salome in 1950.
[43] The Magic and the Commitment by Joyce Trisler. Dance Perspectives 31 (1967) Page 60

Applying the principals on and off stage.

For most serious students of dance, the studio is the preparation for the stage. It is the space where goals are set, theories executed, risks taken and fears overcome. The stage provides performance experience, emotional challenges, mental focus and complete exhilaration. I often have to remind students that they are not training to become professional class takers, as there is a tendency to dance for oneself in a mirror. I will never forget my first experience of Horton at the old Alvin Ailey Studios on 61st and 10th Avenue in New York City. The air was electric with the smell of sweat. I felt as if I was dancing on holy ground, stained with the blood, sweat and tears of countless dancers who were fighting for what I wanted, the stage.

I had never experienced such adrenalin, my first class was with Ana-Marie Forsythe, with live percussion by Victor See-Yeun and from the moment we started the roll down, I felt I was on stage, pouring my heart out to an audience of hundreds. Whether it was my excitement and awe at being there, or the passionate way Ana taught and Victor played, Horton propelled me forward as a performer.

Subsequently I have moved ahead in my career, performing in a variety of styles and techniques, with a variety of companies and choreographers, and have never forgotten that first taste of Horton. I have taught countless Horton classes to students and professionals all over the world, and it never ceases to amaze me how dynamic, energetic and creative the technique has become.

As a performer, I have discovered that through my exposure to Horton, and the principal that it was designed to be performed, I have been encouraged to think outside the room, and the stage- I learnt the importance of physical presence not only onstage, but in everyday life. The Horton technique is a bold and hungry technique, it eats up space both physically and in focus and by being clear with its intention and goals, it leaves room for the development of the artist. I have found it useful to clarify the performance goal in each exercise of the technique, so as to expose the outcome of each movement and initiation. This allowed me to become aware when entering a room, of filling it with my energy and physical consciousness.

An exercise I often employ is to change the position of the imaginary audience in the room. By placing them behind and on either side of the dancers, it seems to deepen there understanding of the dimensions of the body and has the potential to increase body confidence and sensitivity to the surrounding space. To encourage visual interaction between the dancers, I often divide the class into two groups and have them face one another, this I find creates personal connections that are integral in developing partnering and artistry, as well as providing a focus goal that does not always revolve around the dancers own experience, but gives them an opportunity to observe someone else's process.

What I have always heard from audience members when meeting me after a performance, is that I appeared much taller and broader on stage- this again I think is attributed to the illusion of length and the focus of the energy through the body, which is not limited by the physical end of the limb, but is infinite in its energetic reach. This lengthening I have noticed also creates a feeling of suspension, and it seems as if the body is constantly prepared to act and react. I have used the image of boiling lava, positioned within the center of the body, it is constantly simmering, prepared to explode. From the moment the dancer steps into class, or on stage, this simmering of energy is turned on, and the body is prepared to act and initiate depending on the demands of the choreography. There is never a "dead moment" in the movement, even when a shape is achieved, the opportunity for growth and length within that shape is infinite, therefore the body is never unbalanced nor able to fatigue for the opposing energies and lengthening qualities keep the muscles active.

Horton's own investigation of movement was not safe and I have always encouraged my students and dancers to fall, to take risks and develop or explore their own limitations. Only by falling do we become aware of our own limitations and learn about how to strengthen our weaknesses, and harness our strengths. Sarah Stackhouse[44], a veteran Limón dancer has often said to me," Without falls, there can be no recoveries[45]".

---

[44] Sarah Stackhouse danced with José Limón Company from 1958 to 1969 as a principal dancer and partner to José Limón. She has also danced with the Alvin Ailey American Dance Theater and Louis Falco and Dancers.
[45] During a rehearsal for Limon's solo Chaconne, Sadlers Wells London April 2008

It is important as the students begin to develop and have a solid understanding of the technique that individuality in artistic interpretation is encouraged, this can be achieved by asking them to play in the music, in other words, have them experiment with the rhythms, accents and lyrical versus percussive qualities. Altering the musical quality of the exercises can further develop the dynamic variations already designed within the technique. By having the dancers execute a combination slowly, with an adagio feeling, then again with a faster more percussive quality they may better understand the importance of dynamic variation in creating a dynamic vocabulary. As in any language, the words, and the structure of a paragraph become dull and unexpressive without grammar, basic comas, apostrophes, full stops and exclamation marks, provide a clearer intention and a more expressive conversation. I feel dynamics are the grammar of dance vocabulary, the more variations and decisions made in the insertion of suspensions, stops, pulls and pushes of energy and movement, the more powerful and expressive the movement becomes, much like poetry.

"What are the possibilities"? This is a question I ask continually during a class or a rehearsal, it encourages my own, and certainly the students creativity, and propels their performance forward, not only as a dancer, but also a choreographer, I ask them to think about where the movement has come from, and where they think it could go, much like Horton's own tool for developing his work.

In an excerpt from an interview[46] with James Truitte, an ex Horton Company member said of Horton in class," I have seen him stop people in class and ask them, 'Who are you'? If you are you, don't try to dance like him or her, dance like yourself. He told us, 'Your own personal individuality is your most priceless asset'. Lester did not want to make little Lester Horton's of us".

Thanks to Alvin Ailey, the work of Lester Horton has been performed all over the world. His technique is taught widely, and there is more interest in him now then when he was alive. Many of his dancers are respected performers, teachers and choreographers. Joyce Trisler recalls, " I wish I could understand what Lester was trying to do for us at the time. I didn't. I resented him as much as I

---

[46] Interview between Larry Warren and James Truitte in NYC, June 3rd 1973.

loved him. He challenged me both physically and mentally, more than anyone I have known before or since. I fought with him constantly, and was almost thrown out of the company on several occasions. Not until years later did I understand what he was trying to say: " The commitment is total, or not at all".[47]

---

[47] The Magic and the Commitment by Joyce Trisler. Dance Perspectives, 31 (1967). Page 64

The Future of Horton

Considering the Horton technique is a relatively young and possibly less known of the American modern techniques, it is remarkably refined and developed in its structure and functions. Certainly in the last 10 years, there has been an increase in its demand in schools and academies throughout the world. There is an annual Horton summit held in California in the USA headed by Don Martin as well as an annual Horton Pedagogy workshop held at The Ailey School in New York City, run by Ana Marie Forsythe, and covering all aspects of the technique including changes to teaching styles and explorations and new developments within the exercises themselves. These workshops allow teachers of the technique an opportunity to communicate and gain a better network for spreading the word about the Horton Technique. It seems there is always room to explore and cultivate new ideas and goals within the Horton principals, I am sure this was intentional on the part of Mr. Horton, who's own foundation has been strengthened and built on by a generation of teachers who, as I do, see its potential.

Today, professional companies in the United States who still use the technique as a training tool include; The Alvin Ailey American Dance Theater, Philadanco, Dayton Contemporary Dance Company, Dallas Black Dance Theater and Cleo Parker Robinson Dance Company and Lines Ballet in San Francisco, USA. There are also a number of smaller companies with artistic directors who are Horton trained and influenced by the Horton Technique, these include Freddie Moor's, Footprints, Karen Arceneaux's, Genesis Dance Company and Doorknob Company under the direction of former Ailey Dancers, Toni Pierce and Yuri Sands, based in Minnesota

The Future of Horton remains in the hands of those who believe in upholding the integrity of its principals and who see the endless possibilities and creativity it can bring. Ana Marie Forsythe has said to me on more than one occasion that the Horton technique was given to her as a gift, it is clear that the joy and passion from which it was created will continue to flourish long into the future. The idea that it has, and will continue to develop long past its creator's death, is an inspiration for generations of dancers to come.

CHAPTER 5
CHOREOGRAPHIC WORKS

Choreographic Works by Lester Horton

Unless otherwise specified, all costumes, choreography, scores and decors were by Lester Horton. Theaters were in Los Angeles unless otherwise noted. Percussion scores were arranged by William Bowne and Horton and the program credit was given most frequently only for the choreographer.

July 1, 1928. *Argus Bowl.*

THE SONG OF HIAWATHA

Music by: Various composers

September 2, 1929. *Argus Bowl.*

SIVA-SIVA

Music by: Sol Cohen

August 28th, 1931. *Argus Bowl.*

KOOTENAI WAR DANCE

Music: Percussion

August 8th, 1932. *Philharmonic Auditorium.*

VOODOO CEREMONIAL

Music: Percussion Score

Décor: Albert Deano

September 1932. *Little Theater of the Ver∂ugos.*

TAKWISH THE STAR MAKER

Music: Roland Klump

Décor: Jean Abel

Costumes: Jean Able and Lester Horton

July 1933. *Little Theater of the Ver∂ugos.*

ORIENTAL MOTIFS

Music: Percussion score

January 19th, 1934. *Wilshire-Ebell Theater.*

ALLEGRO BARBARO

Music: Béla Bartók

MAY NIGHT

Music: Selim Palmgren

February 23, 1934. *Little Theater of the Ver∂ugos.*

HAND DANCE

Music: Polynesian (percussion)

LAMENT

Music: Hebrew

SALOME

Décor: William Kline

Costumes: Portia Woodbury

July 25, 1934. *Shrine Auditorium.*

Incantation from *ABORIGINAL SUITE*

Music: Percussion score

DANCES OF THE NIGHT

TWO ARABESQUES

Music: Eric Satie

DANSE CONGO

Music: T. Masarachia

SALOME

Music: Constance Boynton

Costumes: "Portia"

August 8, 1934. *Shrine Auditorium.*

AZTEC BALLET

Music: Percussion score (Brahm Van den Berg)

Décor: Jean Abel

Costumes: Jean Abel, Lester Horton

SECOND GNOSSIENNE

Music: Eric Satie

CONCERTO GROSSO, 2nd movement

Music: Ernest Bloch

PAINTED DESERT BALLET

Music: Homer Grunn

Costumes: Portia Woodbury, Lester Horton

October 26th, 1934. *Shrine Auditorium.*

CHINESE FANTASY

Music: Percussion score

November 30th, 1934. *Philharmonic Auditorium.*

BOLERO

Music: Maurice Ravel

Costumes: Jaron de St. Germain

December 11th, 1934. *Tuesday Afternoon Club of Glendale*

AVE

Music: Zoltán Kodály

MAIDENS

SALUTATION

Music: Dane Rudhyar

GNOSSIENNE #3

Music: Eric Satie

VALE

Music: Zoltán Kodály

February 22,1935. *Philharmonic Auditorium.*

MOUND BUILDERS (revision of *AZTEC BALLET*)

Music: Sidney Cutner

Costumes: Elizabeth Talbot-Martin and group

PASSACAGLIA

Music: Otto Respighi

PENTECOST

Music: Dane Rudhyar

DICTATOR

Music: Sidney Cutner

RAIN QUEST

Music: Bertha English

Costumes: "Portia"

May 24,1935. *Long Beach Masonic Temple.*

CONFLICT

RITUAL AT MIDNIGHT

Music: Constance Boyton

TENDRESSE

Music: Krien

June 25,1935. *Occidental Bowl, Occidental College.*

SUN RITUAL

Music: Bertha English

July 31,1935. *Brunswig Gardens (private estate)*

RHYTHMIC DANCE

Music: Alexandre Tansman

SALUTATION TO THE DEPTHS

Music: Dance Rudhyar

December 10, 1935. *Figueroa Playhouse.*

THE MINE

Music: Sidney Cutner

Costumes: Elizabeth Talbot-Martin, Jaron de St. Germain

THE ART PATRONS

Music: Sidney Cutner

Costumes: Elizabeth Talbot-Martin, Jaron de St. Germain

March 21,1936. *Figueroa Playhouse.*

GROWTH OF ACTION

Music Dane Rudhyar

TWO DANCES FOR A LEADER

Music: Sidney Cutner

FLIGHT FROM REALITY

Music: Dane Rudhyar

LYSISTRATA

Music: Sidney Cutner

July 15, 1936. *Hollywood Concert Hall.*

CEREMONY (revision of SUN RITUAL)

Music: Bertha English

January 17, 1937. *Pasadena Playhouse.*

PRELUDE TO MILITANCY

Music: Riccardo Malipiero

CHRONICLE

Music: Sidney Cutner

April 26, 1937. *Philharmonic Auditorium.*

SALOME (revision)

Music: Bertha English

PROLOGUE TO AN EARTH CELEBRATION

Music: Heitor Villa-Lobos

Art Direction: William Bowne

EXHIBITION DANCE NUMBER 1

Music: Bertha Miller English

Art Direction: William Bowne

August 5, 1937. *Hollywood Bowl.*

LE SACRED U PRINTEMPS

Music: Igor Stravinsky

Costumes: William Bowne

October 1, 1937. *Greek Theater.*

SALOME (revision)

Music: Bertha Miller English

Costumes: Jaron de St, Germain

April 24, 1938. *San Francisco Community Playhouse*

PASAREMOS

Music: Bertha Miller English

HAVEN

Music: Bertha Miller English

August 5, 1938. *Mills College.*

CONQUEST

Music: Lou Harrison

Décor: Lou Harrison, Lester Horton

Costumes: Dorothy Gillanders

February 17, 1939. *Wilshire- Ebell-Theater*

DEPARTURE FROM THE LAND

Music: Gerhardt Dorn

Art Direction: Robert Tyler Lee

FIVE WOMEN

Music: Gerhardt Dorn

November 3, 1939. *Philharmonic Auditorium.*

SOMETHING TO PLEASE EVERYBODY

Music: Lou Harrison

¡TIERRA Y LIBERTAD!

Music: Gerhardt Dorn

Décor and costumes: William Bowne

July 6, 1940. *Mills College.*

SIXTEEN TO TWENTY-FOUR

Music: Lou Harrison

November 15, 1940. *Wilshire-Ebell Theater.*

A NOBLE COMEDY (revision of *LYSISTRATA*)

Music: Simon Abel

May 26, 1941. *Assistance League Playhouse.*

PAVANNE

Music: William Byrd

Costumes: Hazel Roy Butler

December 13, 1947. *Philharmonic Auditorium.*

BARREL HOUSE

Music: Anita Short Metz

May 22, 1948. *Dance Theater.*

TOTEM INCANTATION

Music: Judith Hamilton

Décor and Costumes: William Bowne

THE BELOVED

Music: Judith Hamilton

SALOME (revision)

Music: percussion score

Décor: William Bowne

March 5, 1949. *Dance Theater.*

WARSAW GHETTO

Music: Sol Kaplan

Décor and Costumes: Keith Finch

THE PARK

Music: dialogue by Sonia Brown and street sounds

Décor: William Bowne

THE BENCH OF THE LAMB

Music: Mary Hoover

A TOUCH OF KLEE AND DELIGHTFUL TWO

Music: Camargo Guanieri

Décor and costumes: Lewis Brown

March 21, 1949. *Las Palmas Theater.*

TONGUE IN CHEEK

Musical review staged by Bella Lewitzky and Lester Horton

January 19, 1950. *Dance Theater.*

ESTILO DE TU

Music: Aaron Copland, Kenneth Klaus, Milton Rosen

Décor: Lewis Brown

Costumes: Judith Sander, Lester Horton

BOUQUET FOR MOLLY

Music: Earl Robinson

Décor and costumes: Lewis Brown

EL REBOZO

Music: Mary Hoover

Décor: William Bowne

Costumes: George Allen, Lester Horton

April 11, 1950. *Dance Theater.*

SALOME (revision)

Music: Percussion score

Décor: William Bowne

July 1950. *Dance Theater.*

BROWN COUNTY, INDIANA

Music: Kenneth Klaus

Décor: William Bowne

Costumes: Rudi Gernreich

RHYTHM SECTION

Music: Percission

March 31, 1951. *Dance Theater.*

TROPIC TRIO

Music: Audree Covington

ON THE UPBEAT

Music: Audree Covington

ANOTHER TOUCH OF KLEE

Music: Stan Kenton

May 26, 1951. *Ojai Festival.*

MEDEA

Music: Audree Covington

July 21, 1951. *Greek Theater.*

GIRL CRAZY

George Gershwin musical.

August 13, 1951. *War Memorial Opera House, San Francisco.*

ANNIE GET YOUR GUN

Irving Berlin Musical

May 23, 1952. *Dance Theater.*

SEVEN SCENES WITH BALLABILLI

Music: Gertrude Rivers Robinson

Costumes: Eleanor Johnson (under the direction of Lester Horton)

LIBERIAN SUITE

Music: Duke Ellington

Accessories: Martha Koerner

PRADO DE PENA

Music: Gertrude Rivers Robinson

Props: Martha Koerner

March 8, 1953. *Wilshire- Ebell Theater.*

DEDICATIONS IN OUR TIME

Music: Gertrude Rivers Robinson.

"To Ruth, Mary and Martha" : cast- Carmen de Lavallade, Sondra Orans, Joyce Trisler; "Memorial to Hiroshima" : cast- Misaye Kawasumi; " To Carson McCullers":

cast- Sondra Orans

Music: Kenneth Klaus. "To José Clemente Orozco" (revision of "Soldadera" from *Estilo de Tu*): cast- Carmen de Lavallade, Jack Dodds; "To Federico Garcia Lorca": cast- Carmen de Lavallade, Joyce Trisler, Norman Cornick, Jack Dodds, James Truitte.

Films Choreographed by Lester Horton: (BY YEAR)

1942

MOONLIGHT IN HAVANNA (Universal-International)

1943

RHYTHM OF THE ISLANDS

WHITE SAVAGE

PHANTOM OF THE OPERA

(all with Universal-International)

1944

CLIMAX (Universal-International)

1945

SALOME, WHERE SHE DANCED

THAT NIGHT WITH YOU

FRISCO SAL

SHADY LADY

(all with Universal-International)

1946

TANGIER (Universal-International)

1948

SIREN OF ATLANTIS (United Artists Release)

1949

BAGDAD (Universal-International)

1953

SOUTH SEA WOMAN (Warner Brothers)

3-D FOLLIES (R.K.O)

List of Illustrations

ABOUT THE AUTHOR

Bradley Shelver was born in East London, South Africa. He started dancing at the age of 4, after being accepted into the Johannesburg based, Performing Arts Workshop, directed by Jeff Corey. He trained extensively in all disciplines and after the Closing of P.A.W in 1987, he continued his training with Delia Sainsbury and Keith Galloway.

He holds his advanced Diplomas in Tap, Jazz and Ballet through the Imperial Society of Teachers of Dancing in London and attended the National School of the Arts in Johannesburg as well as The Ailey School, under a full fellowship from Judith Jameson.

He has danced as a soloist with the companies of **Alvin Ailey Repertory Ensemble (Now Ailey 2), Elisa Monte Dance, Complexions Contemporary Ballet, Ballet Hispanico of New York, Limón Dance Company, Metropolitan Opera Ballet and Phoenix Dance Theater in the UK.**

He has performed as a guest artist with opera Singer, Jesse Norman at Carnegie Hall in 1999, in the off Broadway Musical, " The Making of a Perfect Mate" in 2000 and with companies like; **The Mark Morris Dance Group, Universal Ballet Company, Lar Lubovich Dance Company, New Jersey Dance Theater Ensemble, Eglevsky Ballet, Minnesota Ballet Arts, Bill T. Jones/Arnie Zane Dance and the Francesca Harper Project.** He has also performed with the Radio City Christmas Spectacular.

He has performed works by; Jiri Kylian, Angelin Preljocaj, Ohad Naharin, Alexei Ratmansky, Elisa Monte, William Forsythe, David Brown, Milton Myers, Alvin Ailey, José Limón, Ronald K. Brown, Bill T Jones, to name a few. He was Principal dancer and Singer in **Javier De Frutos'** , "Cattle Call" which has toured around the UK in collaboration with Composer, Richard Thomas.

As a choreographer, He has created Solo and Company works which have premiered in Italy, Israel, Brazil and Denmark, Sweden, United States, South Africa, Israel, Germany and has been featured in International gala's as a solo performer as well as conducting solo tours. He is Co-Producer and Curator for the annual, New york based, **REVERBdance Festival.**

He has written monthly columns for Dance Spirit Magazine as well as numerous online blogs.

He is co-founder and Artistic Director of Bradley Shelver Contemporary Dance Theater founded in 2003.

He is on the Teaching Faculty of: The Alvin Ailey School (NY), Oure Sports School (Denmark), STEPS on Broadway (NYC), Estemporada Academy (Italy) Labart School (Napoli), Ials (Rome), Svenska Balett Skolen (Sweden), London Contemporary Dance School, Millennium School (London) MAS Academy (Milan) as well as conducting master classes and workshops throughout the US, Europe , South America, Israel and Africa. He has taught as company teacher for **Matthew Bourne's 'New Adventures in Motion Pictures'** and **Phoenix Dance Theater (UK).** He has Taught for the Alteballeto Festival in Italy, and the Bartholin Ballet Festival at the Royal Theater in Copenhagen and the Laban Centre in London. As well as for the World Modern Dance Congress in Rio de Janeiro, Brazil.

Made in the USA
Coppell, TX
31 August 2022

82374320R00090